CAST IRON

COOKBOOK

365 DAYS OF EASY ONE PAN RECIPES FOR YOUR CAST IRON SKILLET & DUTCH OVEN

BY FINLEY MACK

TABLE OF CONTENTS

INTRODUCTION

I'd like to welcome each and every one of you that has purchased this book. Whether you're a beginner or you've been cooking for years, this book was created with you in mind. Together with my family, I created this book to help guide you into the wonderful world of cast-iron cooking. Your dinners and Sunday lunches will never be the same again. These recipes have been tried and tested, allowing you the ease and convenience of jumping right in.

There is plenty of advice out there regarding the cleaning and maintenance of your cast-iron pots and pans. Personally, I stick to the ones that have been passed down from generation to generation in our family. In this book, I'll lay them all out for you in a nifty and easy-to-use introduction, because if something isn't broken, why fix it? You will learn all the tips and tricks you will ever need to maintain and lengthen the life of your cast-iron cookware.

Cast-iron definitely has its added share of maintenance compared to normal pots and pans. But don't let that frighten you off, the benefits far outweigh the extra elbow grease. Sealing in all of the flavor and improving the overall quality of your dishes for one.

After a few meals and happy tummies, you may find yourself packing away your regular pots and pans in favor of these. Whether it's a family heirloom from great-grandma or a spur of the moment purchase because of your favorite cooking show, your cast-iron investment is about to pay off in a big way.

You can do so much more than just the traditional dishes. Sit back and be amazed at all of the time you can save with one pot or pan recipes. Not to mention the ease in cleaning up!

Whatever you're trying to cook, allow your cast-iron cookware to seal in the flavor.

HOW TO SEASON CAST-IRON COOKWARE

A brand-new pot or skillet has a rough grainy coating when you run your fingers over the surface. A properly seasoned skillet, however, is smooth and has a darker appearance.

Try to avoid any pots and skillets that have an added enamel coating, this will prevent the oils and fats from bonding with the skillet as you cook over time, eliminating the whole point of properly seasoned cast-iron.

SEASONING YOUR COOKWARE

If you have purchased a brand-new cast-iron piece, your first step is to scrub off the factory coating that usually consists of a paraffin-like substance or shellac. This extra layer is a barrier that will prevent proper seasoning. Begin by scouring your cookware in hot soapy water, you want to get every nook and cranny, including the handle and exterior.

Thoroughly dry the skillet or pot before heating it on a stove top over medium heat, this will get rid of any excess water that has been soaked into the pores. If you notice a chemical smell while heating your skillet or pot, repeat the washing and heating process until it is gone.

Now that the added barrier has been removed, you are ready to season your pot or skillet for the very first time. Set the oven to preheat at 350°F with a large piece of tin foil on the bottom rack.

Use rendered fat to generously coat the exterior and inside of the skillet. Place the skillet upside down on top of your tin foil for an hour. The foil will catch the drippings.

Don't panic if you start to see smoke or smell burning, this is a normal part of the seasoning process. It just means that all of the great flavors are being sealed in!

When the hour is up, turn off the oven. Allow your skillet to cool completely in the oven for 12-24 hours. Your skillet will be a shade darker when it is ready, but not completely black like a well-seasoned one. This blackening will occur over time as you use and maintain the skillet.

PREPPING PRE-SEASONED COOKWARE

If you do not wish to go through all the steps of seasoning an unseasoned skillet and don't mind the price, you can always purchase a pre-seasoned skillet. You will however notice that the price will be significantly higher.

If you do however purchase a pre-seasoned skillet or pan, you can simply wash it with hot water using a Teflon brush and no soap. Once your cookware is completely dry, rub in some sunflower oil using a wadded-up piece of greaseproof paper.

RE-SEASONING YOUR COOKWARE

If you notice a spot of rust or a dent on the seasoned layer of your cookware, don't panic. Cast-iron does not have to be re-seasoned after every use but will require occasional maintenance. Maintenance re-seasoning is just as simple as the first time you seasoned your pot or pan.

- If rust has appeared, you will need to scour your pan with steel wool or sand it down with sand paper if that does not do the trick. After the rust has been removed, simply repeat the steps you used to pre-season.
- If you end up burning the coating, let's be honest it happens to the best of us, use the same process you would to remove rust and then re-season.
- If you notice a spot that appears to be drier than the surrounding coating, scour the pot before re-seasoning and baking. You can repeat the process as many times as it takes to replenish the coat.
- Even without any of the above incidents, your cookware should be re-seasoned about twice a year for optimal use of the coating.

CLEANING CAST-IRON

With the exception of the pre-seasoning when you first purchase your pot or pan, you do not need to use soap when cleaning your cookware. Hot water and a plastic brush is all that is required. Scrubbing with anything more abrasive will definitely remove the coating you have built up.

You may need to adjust the way you clean after every meal, some dishes use different methods of cooking that build up fats and slightly burnt pieces in different ways.

If the dish is excessively fatty, allow the fat to cool completely in the pan before gently removing it under hot water with your plastic brush.

If your food is overly acidic or you've braised a dish, you will want to clean and re-season your pot or pan immediately after use. Food that is burnt or stuck can be removed by adding some salt to the cookware while you scrub it, this is abrasive enough to remove the food without damaging the seasoned layer.

The final step in cleaning after every use is to place it in an oven on low to evaporate any water that may have soaked into the pores. You may also place the pot or pan on the stove. This is essential if you want to prevent rust. Always rub in some oil before storing it in a cupboard.

CAST-IRON STORAGE

Since these pots and pans don't scratch, you can stack them together. You can also hang them from a firmly attached pot rack. Or, you can leave them on the stove top or in the oven, like many cast-iron users do.

If you rarely cook or have to store your cookware for an extended period of time, it's best to coat them lightly in vegetable oil inside and out. It's a good idea to oil newer pots and pans after each use. The oil not only keeps the pans from rusting, it also keeps the oil on the rough surface of the pan from drying up and after time makes the pan easier to clean and cook with.

DOS AND DON'TS

Cast-iron has a bad reputation as far as maintenance is concerned, but as long as you follow these steps, you can avoid all the headaches that come with neglected cookware. It is really not as difficult as everyone makes it out to be.

Do:
- Always oil after every use.
- The water should always be evaporated after every wash.
- Never allow it to stand overnight, clean straight after every use.
- Do not stir caramelizing food, this will inevitably make it stick.
- Preheat your pan before adding oils and fats.
- Never place the heated pots and skillets directly on a counter.

Don't:
- Clean it in a dishwasher.
- Use anything metal to scrape off food.
- Leave it to dry on a rack instead of evaporating with heat.
- Leave it in water to soak.
- Boil water.
- Use it to store food.
- Clean it with chemicals.

NOW LET'S COOK!

These seasoning, cleaning, and cooking tips are all that you need to start using your cookware. A great way to mark the occasion of your very first meal is tackling a super fatty dish. Bacon is usually the answer to everything, so frying something with a lot of bacon will start adding the amazing flavors you want to build up.

These recipes provide a great starting point as you become more acquainted with your cast-iron pieces. Like everything else in life, practice makes perfect, so don't hesitate to try each and every one of these recipes. Don't get overwhelmed if you are not familiar with cast-iron, cooking and caring for your pieces will become second nature it no time at all!

Now heat up that pan and enjoy!

BREAKFAST & BRUNCH

APPLE CINNAMON DUTCH BABY

COOK TIME: 30 MINS | MAKES: 4 SERVINGS

INGREDIENTS:

- 1 small green apple
- 6 tbsp. melted butter
- 1 tbsp. tightly packed, dark brown sugar
- 1/2 tsp. salt
- 3/4 tsp. ground cinnamon
- 2 tsp. vanilla essence
- 2/3 cup all-purpose flour
- 2/3 cup full-cream milk

- 4 large eggs
- 2 tbsp. cold butter
- 1/2 cup honey
- 1/2 tsp. ground cinnamon
- 1/2 tsp. vanilla essence
- whipped cream for serving

DIRECTIONS:

1. Set the oven to preheat at 425°F with the wire rack in the middle of the oven.

2. Clean and core the apple before cutting it into thin slices. Place 3\4 of the sliced apple in a cast-iron skillet and coat the slices with 4 tablespoons of the melted butter. Toss the sugar into the skillet and make sure that the slices are evenly coated. Move the skillet to the oven and cook the apples until all the sugar has melted and the slices are just beginning to brown, about 10 minutes.

3. In a food processor, combine 1\2 teaspoon salt, 3\4 teaspoon cinnamon, 2 teaspoons vanilla essence, 2\3 cups flour, and 4 eggs. Pulse until the mixture is lump-free.

4. Carefully remove the skillet from the oven and drizzle the lump-free mixture over the baked apples. Move the skillet back to the oven for 18-20 minutes. The Dutch baby is ready when it has grown to more than half the size of the batter that was poured into the pan. It's important that you don't open the oven for the first 15 minutes as this may stop the batter from rising.

5. Meanwhile, in a cast-iron pot over high heat, combine the 2 tablespoons butter, 1\2 cup honey, and 1\2 teaspoon of ground cinnamon. Stir until everything is properly combined. Remove the pot from the heat and stir in the 1\2 teaspoon of vanilla essence. Place the lid on the cast-iron pot to keep the honey warm.

6. When the Dutch baby is ready, remove the skillet from the oven and arrange the remaining apple slices in the center. Drizzle with the warm honey and dollop generously with the whipped cream if desired.

BAKED ITALIAN PROSCIUTTO EGGS

COOK TIME: 6 MINS | MAKES: 1 SERVING

INGREDIENTS:

- 1 tbsp. butter
- 1 slice prosciutto
- 2 tbsp. tomato puree
- 2 extra-large eggs
- 1/3 tsp. Italian herb blend
- salt

- pepper
- 1 tbsp. heavy cream
- 1/3 cup mozzarella
- 1 tsp. freshly chopped chives, for seasoning.

DIRECTIONS:

1. Set the oven to preheat at 350°.

2. Use a small cast-iron frying pan to melt the butter on the stove and set aside.

3. Place the prosciutto in the melted butter and top with the puree, using the back of a tablespoon to spread it around.

4. Gently crack the eggs over the tomato prosciutto, taking care not to damage the yolks. Sprinkle the eggs with the Italian herb blend and a pinch of salt and pepper.

5. Carefully pour the cream over the seasoned eggs and top with the cheese.

6. Move the skillet to the oven and cook the eggs for 5-6 minutes or until the whites are no longer runny. Garnish the eggs with chives and serve immediately in the pan.

SPICY POTATO WRAPS

COOK TIME: 35-40 MINS | MAKES: 6-8 SERVINGS

INGREDIENTS:

- 2 cups extra virgin olive oil
- 1 shallot
- 2 large potatoes
- 8 large eggs
- Himalayan salt

- 1/3 tsp. cayenne pepper
- 1 tsp. paprika
- 1 tsp. crushed garlic
- 1 lemon, juiced
- 1/2 cup tangy mayonnaise

DIRECTIONS:

1. Use a cast-iron pan to gradually heat the oil over low heat on the stove.

2. Peel and slice both the shallot and potato into thin slices. Add them to the heated oil and allow them to cook for 2o-25 minutes or until they are just beginning to soften.

3. Transfer the cooked shallot and potato slices to a bowl, strain any excess oil. Set aside two tablespoons of the oil in a small bowl.

4. In a large bowl, beat the eggs until they are light and foamy. Add the cooked vegetables, salt, and cayenne pepper, stirring gently until everything is combined.

5. Use one tablespoon of the oil from earlier to once again heat the pan over medium heat. Gently transfer the eggs from the bowl into the pan with the vegetables. Allow the eggs to cook until they are no longer runny, 7-10 minutes. Once the eggs are cooked, take the pan off the stove and set aside on a potholder or wooden chopping board.

6. While the eggs are resting in the pan, place the paprika, crushed garlic, lemon juice, mayonnaise, and a pinch of salt in a medium bowl. Beat until everything is combined and you have a creamy dressing.

7. Use a pot lid that fits your pan to cover the top of the eggs, turn the pan upside down, and carefully set the eggs aside. Use the remaining tablespoon of oil and heat the pan. Once the oil is hot, return the eggs to the pan and cook for an extra 5 minutes.

8. When your egg wrap is nice and browned, turn it out onto a plate. Top with your creamy dressing and serve.

ITALIAN PAN OMELETTE

COOK TIME: 35 MINS | MAKES: 1 LARGE OMELETTE

INGREDIENTS:

- 2 tbsp. olive oil
- 3-4 lb. spicy sausage, chopped
- 1 cup heavy cream
- 6 large eggs
- 1/3 tsp. salt
- 1/3 tsp. pepper

- 13 tsp. cayenne pepper
- 2 cups kale, washed and chopped
- 1 tomatillo, husk removed and chopped
- 8 oz. feta cheese

DIRECTIONS:

1. Set the oven to preheat at 375°.

2. In a cast-iron pan, heat the olive oil over medium heat. Add the chopped sausage and use a wooden spoon to mix until the sausage is properly cooked. Transfer the sausage to a bowl lined with kitchen towels. Remove any excess oil from the pan, leaving a very thin layer to coat the bottom.

3. In a large bowl, beat the cream, eggs, salt, pepper, and cayenne pepper until the mixture is light and frothy. Mix in the kale, tomatillo, feta cheese, and cooked sausage.

4. Transfer the mixture to the pan and cook until the eggs are no longer runny. Transfer the skillet to the oven for 25-30 minutes or until your omelet is nicely browned.

5. Cut and serve straight away.

GERMAN CARAMELIZED ONION PANCAKE

COOK TIME: 35 MINS | MAKES: 4 SERVINGS

INGREDIENTS:

- 1 large onion
- 2 tbsp. extra virgin olive oil
- 1 tbsp. flour
- 2 tbsp. white wine
- 1/2 cup beef stock
- 1/8 tsp. salt
- 1/8 tsp. pepper

- 2 tsp. crushed thyme
- 3 tbsp. butter
- 4 large eggs
- 1/2 cup full-cream milk
- 1/3 tsp. salt
- 1/2 cup all-purpose flour
- watercress, roughly chopped for garnish

DIRECTIONS:

1. Peel and slice the onion into thin strips. Heat the olive oil in a cast-iron pan over medium heat before adding the sliced onion. Place a lid over the pan and allow the onion slices to cook for 15 minutes. Use a wooden spoon to stir the onions every few minutes. After 15 minutes, remove the cover and allow the onions to simmer over a lower heat until the onions are nicely browned.

2. Stir in the flour until it's properly combined. Add the wine and allow the sauce to simmer for 30 seconds before stirring in your beef stock. Stir throughout. Once your mixture has thickened, add the salt, pepper, and thyme. Transfer the pan to a potholder or wooden chopping board.

3. Meanwhile, set the oven to preheat at 425°F.

4. Use an 8" cast-iron pan to melt the butter over medium heat. Move the pan around so that the butter coats the bottom in an even layer, then set the pan aside.

5. Whisk the eggs in a medium bowl until they are light and fluffy. Add the milk, salt, and flour and continue to whisk until you have a thick batter.

6. Carefully pour your batter over the melted butter and transfer the pan to the oven for 15 minutes or until the pancake is nice and puffy and starting to brown.

7. When your pancake is ready, pour the caramelized onion sauce over it and garnish with the watercress before serving.

CHEESY POACHED EGGS SHAKSHUKA

COOK TIME: 5 MINS | MAKES: 6 SERVINGS

INGREDIENTS:

- 1 1/2 tsp. paprika
- 6 garlic cloves, crushed
- 2 tbsp. extra virgin olive oil
- 1 lb. spinach, cleaned and chopped
- Himalayan salt
- 1/2 cup chicken broth
- black pepper
- cayenne pepper
- 1/2 lemon, juiced

- 4 oz. feta cheese
- 6 large eggs
- 1/2 tsp. oregano
- 1/2 tsp. thyme
- 1 tbsp. toasted sesame seeds
- plain, unsweetened yogurt
- chopped parsley for garnish

DIRECTIONS:

1. Set the oven to preheat at 350°F.

2. Use a Dutch oven over medium heat to cook the paprika and garlic in the olive oil for about 30 seconds before gradually adding the chopped spinach. If the spinach does not fit properly, allow portions to reduce before adding more. Season with salt to taste and continue to stir until all the spinach has wilted. About 7-9 minutes.

3. Add the chicken broth and allow the spinach to simmer for 5 minutes. Stir in a pinch each of the black pepper and cayenne pepper along with the lemon juice before crumbling the cheese over the spinach and mixing.

4. Remove the Dutch oven from the heat and use a wooden spoon to make 6 pockets in the spinach, each big enough for a single egg. Gently crack each egg into its own pocket, taking care not to break the yolks.

5. Place the pot in the oven without the lid. Bake the eggs for about 12 minutes or until the whites are firm.

6. Remove the pot from the oven and sprinkle the eggs evenly with the oregano, thyme, and toasted sesame seeds. Dollop the yogurt over each egg and garnish with parsley before serving.

CRISP ITALIAN BREAKFAST TART

COOK TIME: 40 MINS | MAKES: 6 SERVINGS

INGREDIENTS:

- extra virgin olive oil
- 1/3 tsp. cayenne pepper
- 1/2 tsp. salt
- 1 tbsp. active dry yeast
- 1/4 cup warm water
- 2 cups bread flour, plus extra for dusting
- 1/4 cup full-cream milk
- 8 eggs

- 1 shallot, chopped
- 2 tsp. crushed garlic
- 2 cups baby tomatoes, halved
- 1 cup basil, chopped, plus extra for garnish
- salt
- pepper
- 1/2 cup feta, crumbled

DIRECTIONS:

1. Use 1 tablespoon of olive oil to grease a large bowl. You can simply turn the bowl to coat or use a scrunched-up piece of greaseproof paper to spread the oil.

2. In a separate bowl, whisk together 2 tablespoons of olive oil, cayenne pepper, salt, instant yeast, and warm water. Set the bowl aside and allow the yeast to bloom. Once the yeast has bloomed, use a wooden spoon and gradually stir in the flour until it all comes together.

3. Lightly flour your work surface. Knead the dough until it forms a smooth, elastic ball. About 5-7 minutes. Transfer the dough to your coated bowl and cover the bowl with a damp tea towel. Allow the dough to rise for approximately 1 hour or until the dough has doubled in size. The dough will rise better in a warm area with no drafts.

4. Set the oven to preheat at 350°F.

5. In a large bowl, beat the milk and eggs before adding the shallot, garlic, tomatoes, and a pinch of salt and pepper.

6. Use a cast-iron pan that has been lightly greased with olive oil. Press the dough into the pan using your fingers or the bottom of a glass. Make sure some of the dough goes up the sides to form a border.

7. Pour the egg mixture into the prepared crust and sprinkle the top with feta.

8. Use a basting brush to lightly coat the edges of the dough with olive oil before placing the pan in the oven and baking for about 40 minutes or until the filling has set and the edges are browned.

9. Garnish with the extra basil and serve hot or cold.

FLUFFY GERMAN PANCAKE

COOK TIME: 15 MINS | MAKES: 4 SERVINGS

INGREDIENTS:

- 3 tbsp. butter
- 1/4 tsp. salt
- 1 tsp. almond essence
- 2 tbsp. raw honey
- 1/2 cup full-cream milk

- 1/2 cup all-purpose flour
- 4 large eggs
- maple syrup, for serving
- confectioner's sugar, for serving

DIRECTIONS:

1. Set the oven to preheat at 425°F.

2. Place the butter in a cast-iron frying pan and melt the butter on the stove. Set aside for later.

3. Whisk together the salt, almond essence, honey, milk, flour, and eggs in a large bowl.

4. Drizzle the batter into the skillet with melted butter and place the skillet in the oven for 15 minutes or until the pancake has puffed up to twice the size of the batter. Try not to open the oven for the first few minutes, as this may prevent the batter from rising.

5. Once the pancake is ready sprinkle the confectioner's sugar over the pancake and top with maple syrup. Serve immediately.

ZESTY CREAM CHEESE CREPES

COOK TIME: 4 MINS | MAKES: 12 CREPES

INGREDIENTS:

- 1/2 tsp. salt
- 1/2 tsp. baking soda
- 2 tsp. baking powder
- 2 tbsp. brown sugar
- 2 cups all-purpose flour
- 2 large eggs, whites, and yolks separated

- 1/2 cup plain cream cheese
- 1 1/2 cups full-cream milk
- 1 lemon, zested
- sunflower oil
- raw honey

DIRECTIONS:

1. In a large bowl, whisk together the salt, baking soda, baking powder, brown sugar, and flour. Set aside.

2. In a separate bowl, use a hand or stand mixer to whisk the egg whites until they form soft peaks.

3. In a third bowl, whisk together the egg yolks, cream cheese, and milk until properly combined. Use a wooden spoon to gently incorporate the cream cheese batter into the first bowl with the flour and mix until you have a lump-free batter. Very carefully fold your egg whites and lemon zest into your batter. Take your time as you want the white to retain most of its texture. There should be no visible whites when the batter is ready. It will no longer be lump-free once the whites are incorporated.

4. Heat a cast-iron skillet over medium heat. Place a cup of sunflower oil next to the stove as you may want to grease the pan after every few crepes

5. Once the skillet is hot. Coat the bottom with about a teaspoon of oil. Pour about half a cup of batter into the skillet per crepe. Gently move the pan around to evenly distribute the batter. Bake each crepe for approximately 2 minutes on either side. They should be just golden. Repeat until all the batter is finished.

6. You can keep the crepes warm in a moderate oven until they are ready to be served. Drizzle with honey and enjoy!

POACHED EGGS IN HEARTY MUSHROOM STEW

COOK TIME: 60 MINS | MAKES: 4 SERVINGS

INGREDIENTS:

- Butter
- 3 tsp. crushed garlic
- 6 cups button mushrooms cleaned, and quartered
- 3 tbsp. White wine
- 1/4 tsp. cayenne pepper
- 1/4 tsp. salt
- 1/2 tsp. black pepper
- 1/2 tsp. crushed fennel seeds
- 14 1/2 oz. baby tomatoes, chopped

- 15 0z. tomato puree
- 4 large eggs
- 3 cups full-cream milk
- 1 cup dry polenta
- 1/4 tsp. black pepper
- 1/2 tsp. salt
- 1 lemon, juiced
- 1/4 cup fresh parsley, plus more for garnish
- 1/4 cup parmesan, grated
- 1/4 cup chevre cheese, grated

DIRECTIONS:

1. Set the oven to preheat at 400°F. Coat a 10" cast-iron baking dish with a thick layer of butter and set aside for later.

2. In a cast-iron pan over medium heat, melt 2 tablespoons of butter before adding the garlic and mushrooms. Fry for about 10 minutes or until the mushrooms have darkened.

3. Stir in the wine and allow the mushrooms to marinate for about 30 seconds before adding the cayenne pepper, salt, black pepper, fennel seeds, baby tomatoes, and tomato puree. Lower the heat and allow the sauce to cook for approximately 20 minutes. Stirring after every few minutes.

4. Meanwhile, in a separate pot, heat the milk until it is just starting to boil. Add the polenta and use a whisk to beat the milk until it thickens. Add the pepper, salt, lemon juice, parsley, parmesan, and chevre. Stirring everything through.

5. Pour the mixture into your prepared pan and use an offset spatula to smooth it out. Pour the mushroom stew over the polenta mixture and use the same spatula to spread it out.

6. Use a wooden spoon to make four evenly spaced pockets in the layer of stew. Gently crack each egg into its own pocket, taking care not to damage the yolks.

7. Cover with tinfoil and place the pan in the oven for 30 minutes before removing the foil and baking for an additional 10-12 minutes or until the eggs are no longer runny.

8. Sprinkle with the remaining parsley and serve.

SPICY MEXICAN BREAKFAST TOSS

COOK TIME: 20 MINS |MAKES: 4 SERVINGS

INGREDIENTS:

- 2 tbsp. butter
- 2 tbsp. extra virgin olive oil
- 6 corn tortillas, shredded into 1/2" strips
- 1 shallot, diced
- 1 green chili, seeded and diced
- 2 tsp. crushed garlic
- 1/4 cup heavy cream
- 6 eggs

- 1/4 tsp. Himalayan salt
- 1/4 tsp. cayenne pepper
- 1/4 cup mozzarella, shredded
- 1/4 cup pepper jack cheese, shredded
- 1/2 cup coriander leaves, chopped

DIRECTIONS:

1. In a cast-iron pan over medium heat, melt the butter and stir in the olive oil. Sprinkle your shredded tortillas into the butter and allow them crisp for approximately 5 minutes. Use a wooden spoon to toss them throughout.

2. Turn down the heat before adding the shallot, chili, and garlic powder and browning them with the tortilla strips for about 4 minutes.

3. Beat the cream, eggs, salt, and pepper in a separate bowl. Pour the mixture into the pan and use a wooden spoon to stir for about 6 minutes.

4. Add the cheese and continue to stir until everything is melted.

5. Plate and garnish with the coriander leaves before serving.

APPLE & PORK PATTIES

COOK TIME: 30-40 MINS | MAKES: 16 PATTIES

INGREDIENTS:

- 3 tbsp. olive oil
- 1 bunch spring onions
- 2 green apples
- 1/2 cup sage leaves, chopped
- 1 1/2 tsp. crushed fennel seeds
- 2 lb. pork, minced
- 3/4 tsp. white pepper
- 1 tbsp. Himalayan salt

DIRECTIONS:

1. Set the oven to preheat at 200°F.

2. In a medium cast-iron pan, heat 1 tablespoon of oil over medium heat.

3. Chop and separate the spring onions into whites and greens. Peel, core, and slice the apples into 1/4 wedges. Add the white part of the onions and the apple wedges to the pan. Cook for 5-8 minutes or until the apples are tender and just starting to caramelize. Remove the pan from the heat and allow the apple wedges to cool for 10 minutes.

4. Use a large bowl to combine the green parts of the spring onions, sage leaves, crushed fennel seeds, minced pork, pepper, and salt with the cooled apple mixture. Divide and form the meat mixture into 16 1/4-inch thick patties.

5. In a clean skillet, heat the remaining 2 tablespoons of oil before frying the patties in batches, about 5 minutes per side. Keep an eye on the heat as you do not want the later batches to burn.

6. You can keep the patties warm in the oven, covered with tin foil, or serve straight away.

HALLOUMI & SPRING ONION OMELETTE

COOK TIME: 16 MINUTES | MAKES: 4 SERVINGS

INGREDIENTS:

- 2 tbsp. olive oil
- 3 tbsp. butter
- 6 spring onions, diced and white parts discarded
- Himalayan salt
- white pepper
- 6 eggs
- 3 oz. halloumi cheese
- 1 tsp. crushed thyme

DIRECTIONS:

1. Set the oven to preheat at 350°F with the wire rack in the middle of the oven.

2. Use a medium cast-iron pan to heat 1 tablespoon of the oil and 2 tablespoons of the butter over medium heat. Add the green parts of the spring onions to the pan once the butter and oil is hot, frying for 6 minutes or until the onions are soft. Season to taste with salt and pepper.

3. Using a large bowl, whisk together the 6 eggs, halloumi, and thyme. Season with a small pinch of salt and pepper before whisking in the fried onions.

4. In a clean pan, heat the remaining oil and butter before adding the egg mixture, tilt the pan so that eggs coat the bottom in an even layer.

5. Fry the omelette for approximately 5 minutes. The edges should be set with the middle being slightly runny. You can gently lift the edges with a spatula to ensure the omelette is not burning. When the edges are set, transfer the pan to the oven for an additional 5 minutes until the center is properly cooked.

6. Allow the omelette to rest for 2 minutes in the pan before transferring to a plate and serving.

POULTRY

PERFECT CHICKEN PIE

COOK TIME: 25-35 MINS| MAKES: 6 SERVINGS

INGREDIENTS:

- 1 cup butter
- 1/2 cup all-purpose flour
- 4 cups chicken broth
- 1/4 cup Madeira
- 4 celery stalks, thinly sliced
- 1 shallot, diced
- 1/2 lb. baby potatoes, cubed (about 1/2" cubes)
- 2 carrots, diced
- 1 1/2 tsp. curry powder

- 1 bay leaf
- pinch of Himalayan salt
- pinch of black pepper
- 1 lb. frozen peas
- 1 1/2 lbs. chicken, cooked and cubed
- 1/2 lb. ready-made puff pastry
- 2 tsp. water
- 1 large egg

DIRECTIONS:

1. Set the oven to preheat at 350°F.

2. In a cast-iron pot over medium heat, melt 1/2 cup butter before using a whisk to beat in the flour. Pour in the chicken broth and Madeira, gently whisking until it starts to thicken. Mix in the celery, shallot, potatoes, carrots, curry powder, bay leaf, salt, and black pepper. Reduce the heat and allow the vegetables to simmer for 10 minutes until properly cooked with the lid on the pot. Remove the bay leaf before stirring in the peas and chicken. Move the pot to a wooden chopping board or potholder.

3. In a small cast-iron skillet, melt the remaining butter and set aside.

4. Lightly flour your work surface and roll your puff pastry into 4 equal circles that are big enough to cover your cast-iron pot with the chicken filling. Using a basting brush, brush the melted butter onto each circle and gently layer them on top of each other. Carefully place your stack of pastry over the pot, sealing the sides to form a lid. Cut a small star into your lid for the steam

5. In a small bowl, beat the water and egg before brushing it over the lid.

6. Place the pot in the oven for 25-35 minutes or until the top is golden brown.

LEMONY CRUMBED CHICKEN BREASTS

COOK TIME: 10 MINUTES | MAKES: 4 SERVINGS

INGREDIENTS:

- 1 tbsp lemon zest
- 1 cup all-purpose flour
- 1/3 tsp. light brown pepper
- 1 tsp. Himalayan salt
- 2 chicken breasts, sliced in half
- 1 tbsp. butter
- 1 tbsp. canola oil

- 1 tsp. crushed Rosemary
- 2 tsp. crushed garlic
- 1 lemon, thinly sliced
- 2 lemons, juiced

DIRECTIONS:

1. Whisk together the lemon zest, flour, pepper, and salt in a medium bowl. Coat the chicken breast evenly with the flour and set aside.

2. In a cast-iron pan, melt the butter and stir in the canola oil before adding the rosemary and garlic. Brown the garlic for approximately 3 minutes.

3. Carefully place your coated chicken breasts in the pan and brown on each side for approximately 4-5 minutes. Transfer the pan to a wooden chopping board.

4. Arrange the lemon slices over the breasts and sprinkle with the lemon juice. Season to taste before serving.

CHICKEN-STIR FRY TORTILLAS

COOK TIME: 15 MINS| MAKES: 4 SERVINGS

INGREDIENTS:

- 1 tbsp. coriander leaves, chopped
- 1 tsp. lime zest
- 2 tbsp. butter softened
- 1 shallot. peeled and thinly sliced
- 3 tsp. crushed garlic
- 1/2 tsp. Himalayan salt
- 1 yellow pepper, seeded and thinly sliced
- 1 red pepper, seeded and thinly sliced
- 1/3 tsp. cayenne pepper
- 1/4 tsp. black pepper
- 1/2 tsp. red pepper flakes
- 1/2 tsp. paprika
- 1 lb. chicken breasts, cut into strips
- 1 tbsp. coconut oil
- 12 corn tortillas

DIRECTIONS:

1. In a glass bowl, whisk together the coriander leaves, lime zest, and softened butter.

2. In a separate bowl, toss together the shallot, garlic, salt, and peppers.

3. In a third bowl, whisk together the cayenne pepper, red pepper flakes, and paprika before tossing in and coating the chicken strips.

4. Use a cast-iron pan over medium heat to melt the coconut oil before adding your chicken and cooking for about 10 minutes. The chicken should be properly cooked. Throw in the vegetables and stir until everything is properly cooked, approximately 5 more minutes.

5. Transfer your pan to a wooden chopping board. Pour the coriander and butter mixture into the pan and allow it to stand for 5 minutes before serving with the corn tortillas.

RED WINE & ROSEMARY CHICKEN

COOK TIME: 20 MINS | MAKES: 6 SERVINGS

INGREDIENTS:

- 1/4 cup butter
- 6 slices thick-cut bacon, cubed
- 3 lbs. chicken, cut into 8 pieces
- 1 tsp. black pepper
- 2 tsp. Himalayan salt
- 2 tbsp. rosemary, chopped
- 4 tsp. crushed garlic

- 1/4 cup red wine vinegar
- 1/2 lemon

DIRECTIONS:

1. Use a cast-iron pan over medium heat to melt the butter before adding the bacon and cooking the cubes until they are crispy.

2. Meanwhile, rub the pepper and salt into the chicken.

3. Once the bacon is crisped, add the chicken to the pan and brown on both sides. Add the rosemary, garlic, and red wine to the pan, mixing with a wooden spoon. Reduce the heat slightly and place a lid over the pan. Allow the chicken to simmer for about 10 minutes until the chicken is properly cooked.

4. Plate and drizzle with lemon before serving.

CHEESY LIME-CHICKEN AND RICE

COOK TIME: 55 MINS | MAKES: 6 SERVINGS

INGREDIENTS:

- 1/2 lime, juiced
- 1/2 tsp. Himalayan salt
- 1/4 tsp. cayenne pepper
- 1/3 tsp. black pepper
- 1 lb. chicken breasts
- 1 tsp. safflower oil
- 1 cup basmati rice, cooked
- 15 oz. black beans
- 1/3 cup coriander leaves, chopped

- 3/4 cups of frozen corn, defrosted
- 4 tsp. crushed garlic
- 1/2 chili, seeded and diced
- 2 cups Monterey jack cheese
- 1/4 cup chicken stock
- 1/2 cup sour cream
- 4 spring onions, diced
- 1 tomato, diced

DIRECTIONS:

1. Set the oven to preheat at 375°F.

2. In a large bowl, whisk together the lime juice, salt, cayenne pepper, and black pepper before tossing in the chicken to coat.

3. Use a cast-iron griddle to heat the oil over medium heat before adding the coated chicken and frying for about 8 minutes or until the chicken is properly cooked.

4. Remove the chicken from the stove, allowing the chicken to cool until it is easy to handle. Cut into 1/2" cubes. Toss the chicken in a bowl with the cooked rice, beans, coriander leaves, corn, crushed garlic, chili, and 1 cup of the cheese.

5. In a separate bowl, beat the chicken stock and sour cream with a pinch of salt and pepper to taste. Pour the cream into the chicken and rice, mixing everything through.

6. Spoon your mixture into a 10" pan, sprinkle with the remaining cheese and bake in the oven for 50-55 minutes. The cheese should form a lovely brown crust.

7. Garnish with your spring onions and tomato before serving.

LEMON & ROSEMARY BUTTERFLIED CHICKEN

COOK TIME: 55 MINS | MAKES: 1 WHOLE CHICKEN

INGREDIENTS:

- 1 whole chicken, backbone removed
- black pepper
- Himalayan salt
- 8 oz. fresh figs, halved
- 1/2 cup chicken broth
- 3 tbsp. balsamic vinegar
- 2 tsp. crushed garlic

- 1 onion, diced
- 1 tsp. crushed thyme
- 1 tbsp. butter, melted

DIRECTIONS:

1. Set the oven to preheat at 425°F with a large cast-iron skillet in the center to warm.

2. Place your deboned chicken on a wooden chopping board, breast-side up. Gently use your hands to press the chicken as flat as possible. Season the flattened chicken with a generous amount of pepper and salt.

3. Remove the skillet from the oven and carefully place the chicken in the center. Return the skillet to the oven for 20 minutes before covering the chicken with tin foil and baking for an additional 20-25 minutes, or until the chicken is properly cooked.

4. Remove the skillet from the oven and carefully slide the chicken onto a plate. Set aside for later.

5. Place the skillet on the stove over medium heat, add the figs, chicken broth, balsamic vinegar, garlic, and onions. Simmer until the figs have softened. Stir in the thyme and butter. Pour the sauce over the chicken and serve.

ZESTY SALSA CHICKEN

COOK TIME: 15 MINS | MAKES: 4 SERVINGS

INGREDIENTS:

- 1/4 cup olive oil, plus 1 tbsp.
- 1/4 cup lime juice, plus 1 tbsp.
- 1 green chili, diced
- 4 chicken breasts
- Himalayan salt
- black pepper
- 1 grapefruit, cut into 4" pieces
- 1 orange, cut into 4" pieces
- 10 baby tomatoes, halved
- 4 spring onions, diced

- 1/2 orange, zested
- 1/2 lime, zested
- 1 tsp. cayenne pepper
- 4 cups spinach, diced and cooked

DIRECTIONS:

1. In a small bowl, whisk together 1/4 cup olive oil, 1/4 cup lime juice, and the diced chili.

2. Massage the chicken breasts with salt and pepper to taste before tossing them in the bowl of lime marinade. Seal the bowl and chill for 30 minutes.

3. To make the salsa, toss together 1 tablespoon olive oil, 1 tablespoon lime juice, grapefruit pieces, orange pieces, tomatoes, spring onions, orange zest, lime zest, and cayenne pepper. Set aside for later.

4. Once your chicken is properly chilled. Heat a 10" cast-iron skillet with olive oil and heat on the stove over medium heat. Shake the excess marinade from the chicken breasts. Place the breasts in the pan and fry each for approximately 5 minutes.

5. Plate the chicken and allow it to rest for an additional 5 minutes.

6. Divide the greens between the plates. Top with salsa and serve.

TURMERIC CHICKEN WITH COCONUT MILK

COOK TIME: 12 MINS | MAKES: 6 SERVINGS

INGREDIENTS:

- 1/2 tsp. salt
- 1/4 tsp. cayenne pepper
- 1 tsp. turmeric powder
- 1 tsp. curry powder
- 1 tsp. crushed garlic
- 1 lemon, juiced
- 1 cup coconut milk

- 2 tbsp. Peanut butter
- 1 lb. chicken breasts, sliced into strips
- 1 tbsp. butter
- 1 cup chicken broth
- 1 cup couscous
- 2 cups spinach, cooked
- coriander leaves for serving

DIRECTIONS:

1. In a large bowl, whisk together the salt, cayenne pepper, turmeric, curry powder, garlic, lemon juice, 1/2 cup coconut milk, and peanut butter. Stir in the chicken strips.

2. Heat a large cast-iron skillet over medium heat and melt the butter before adding the chicken strips and cooking them for 8-10 minutes. The chicken should be properly cooked.

3. Using a separate cast-iron pot over medium heat, combine the chicken broth, couscous, and 1/2 cup coconut milk. Bring to a boil and stir for 2 minutes before removing the pot from the stove and allowing the couscous to absorb the liquid, about 5 minutes.

4. Serve the chicken on a bed of couscous and spinach. Decorate with coriander leaves.

CHEESY STUFFED GARLIC CHICKEN

COOK TIME: 45 MINS | MAKES: 4 SERVINGS

INGREDIENTS:

- 1/4 tsp. cayenne pepper
- 1 shallot, diced
- 3 tsp. crushed garlic
- 4 oz. ricotta cheese
- 4 chicken breasts
- Salt
- pepper
- 2 tbsp. olive oil
- 1/4 cup butter

- 2 tbsp. barbecue sauce
- 2 tbsp. balsamic vinegar
- 1/3 cup parmesan, grated

DIRECTIONS:

1. Set the oven to preheat at 350°.

2. In a medium bowl, mix together the cayenne pepper, 3/4 of the shallot and garlic, and the ricotta cheese.

3. Place the chicken on a wooden chopping board and slice them open on one side like a sandwich. Spoon the ricotta mixture into the slit in even amounts. Close the slit with toothpicks, this will prevent the cheese from spilling out while cooking. Sprinkle the chicken with salt and pepper to taste.

4. Use a large cast-iron pan to heat the oil before searing the stuffed chicken breast for approximately 3 minutes on each side. Use tin foil to carefully cover the pan and bake in the oven for 25 minutes.

5. In a smaller pan over medium heat, melt the butter before adding the remaining garlic and shallot, and frying until the onions are tender. Stir in the vinegar and barbecue sauce until the mixture is simmering. Remove the pan from the heat.

6. Carefully take the chicken out of the oven and pour the sauce over the breasts, top with the parmesan and bake in the oven for 10-15 minutes.

7. Remove the pan from the oven and allow the chicken breasts to rest for 5 minutes before serving.

HONEY & MUSTARD CHICKEN

COOK TIME: 60 MINS | MAKES: 4 SERVINGS

INGREDIENTS:

- 1 tbsp. butter
- 3 tsp. crushed garlic
- 1/4 tsp. black pepper
- 1 tsp. salt
- 1/2 tsp. paprika
- 4 chicken thighs
- 1 tbsp. olive oil

- 7 cups pumpkin, peeled and cut into 1/2" cubes
- 2 tbsp. French mustard
- 1/4 cup buttermilk
- 2 tbsp. raw honey
- 1 tsp. crushed rosemary
- 2 tbsp. parsley, chopped

DIRECTIONS:

1. Use one tablespoon of butter to generously coat the inside of a 10" cast-iron baking dish and set the oven to preheat at 400°F.

2. Whisk together the garlic, pepper, salt, and paprika in a small bowl. Place the chicken thighs on a wooden chopping board and use the garlic and spice mixture to coat the chicken in an even layer while you massage the chicken with your fingers.

3. With a cast-iron pan over medium heat, warm the oil before adding the chicken and searing the sides, five minutes on each side.

4. Place half of the pumpkin into the buttered baking dish before placing the seasoned chicken on top and covering the chicken with the rest of the pumpkin. Use tin foil to tent the dish and bake in the oven for 30 minutes. After 30 minutes, remove the tent and return the dish to the oven for an extra 2o minutes or until the chicken is properly cooked through.

5. Remove the dish from the oven and set aside while you make the sauce.

6. In a small glass bowl, whisk together the mustard, buttermilk, honey, rosemary, and 1 tablespoon of the parsley.

7. Arrange the chicken on plates with the pumpkin served on the side. Use a basting brush to coat the chicken in the honey and mustard sauce. Finally, top the chicken with the remaining parsley and serve.

CURRIED CHICKEN MARAQ

COOK TIME: 30 MINS | MAKES: 4 SERVINGS

INGREDIENTS:

- 1 tsp. turmeric powder
- 1 tsp. ground cinnamon
- 2 tsp. ground ginger
- 1 tsp. ground cilantro seeds
- 4 chicken breasts
- 2 tbsp. olive oil
- 4 tsp. garlic cloves, finely chopped
- 1 shallot, sliced and rings separated
- 2 tsp. parsley, chopped
- 2 tsp. cilantro leaves, chopped
- Himalayan salt
- freshly ground black pepper

- 1/2 tsp. saffron threads
- 3/4 cups water
- 1 lemon, juiced
- zest from 1 lemon
- 1/2 cup, dark brown olives, pips removed
- cooked couscous for serving

DIRECTIONS:

1. In a small bowl, whisk together the turmeric, cinnamon, ginger, and ground cilantro seeds. Place the chicken breasts in a bowl and coat the chicken with your spice mixture. Allow the chicken to rest in the fridge while you prepare the rest of the dish.

2. In a large cast-iron pot, heat the oil over medium-high heat before adding the chopped garlic cloves and sliced shallot and frying until the shallot slices have caramelized. Add the seasoned chicken breasts to the pot along with the parsley, and cilantro leaves, stirring occasionally for 3 minutes. Season to taste with salt and pepper.

3. Meanwhile, whisk together the saffron and water before pouring it over the chicken in the pot. Bring the broth to a boil. Once it is boiling, lower the heat and simmer for 15 minutes or until the chicken is properly cooked, stirring occasionally.

4. Add the olives, lemon juice, and zest to the pot. Stir for an additional 5 minutes. Remove the pot from the stove.

5. Serve the maraq immediately on a bed of cooked couscous.

ONE-POT BRAISED DUCK LEGS

COOK TIME: 4 HOURS | MAKES: 6 SERVINGS

INGREDIENTS:

- 6 duck legs
- Himalayan salt
- black pepper
- 1 tbsp. olive oil
- 3 tsp. crushed garlic
- 1 shallot, diced
- 2 celery stalks, chopped (1-inch pieces)
- 4 carrots, chopped (1-inch pieces)

- 2 whole star anise
- 4 thyme sprigs
- 3 cups dried figs, stems removed and sliced
- 2 lb. butternut, peeled and chopped (1-inch pieces)
- 8 cups chicken stock
- 1 tbsp. champagne vinegar
- 2 tbsp. parsley, chopped

DIRECTIONS:

1. Place the duck legs on a wooden chopping board and sprinkle with 1 tablespoon of salt and 1 1/2 teaspoon of pepper.

2. Heat the olive oil in a large cast-iron pot over medium heat. After about 2 minutes, add the duck legs in batches, frying them for about 10 minutes or until the skin is nicely seared. Transfer the legs to a platter and discard most of the oil from the pan.

3. Return the pan to the heat and add the garlic, shallots, celery, and carrots, string for approximately 4 minutes or until the garlic and shallots are just starting to caramelize. Mix in the anise, thyme, figs, and butternut.

4. Carefully add the seared duck legs to the pot around the vegetables. Top with the chicken stock and turn up the heat. Bring the mixture to a boil before stirring in 1 teaspoon of salt and 1/2 teaspoon of pepper. Reduce the heat and allow the pot to simmer with the lid on for 1 1/2-3 hours. Once the duck legs are nice and soft, turn off the plate and allow the legs to marinate in the sauce for 1-30 minutes.

5. Remove any excess fat that may have accumulated on the surface of the pot while the duck was marinating.

6. Plate the vegetables and duck legs using a slotted spoon and set aside.

7. Whisk the vinegar into the sauce before pouring about 1/3 over the duck legs and vegetables. You can serve the remaining sauce on the side. Sprinkle the parsley over the food and serve.

FIERY CUMIN TURKEY BREAST

COOK TIME: 1-2 HOURS| MAKES: 6-8 SERVINGS

INGREDIENTS:

- 1 turkey breast (4-5 lb.)
- 1 tsp. onion powder
- 1 tsp. garlic powder
- 1/2 tsp. cayenne pepper
- 1/2 tsp. white pepper
- 1 tsp. Himalayan salt
- 3 tbsp. ground cumin

- 2 tbsp. vegetable oil
- 1/2 cup chicken broth
- 2 tbsp. flour

DIRECTIONS:

1. Place the turkey breast on a chopping board and remove all of the bones. If you would like a leaner dish, you can remove the skin, but this is not mandatory.

2. In a small glass bowl, whisk together the onion powder, cayenne pepper, white pepper, salt, and cumin. Massage the spice into the turkey breast in an even layer before covering and chilling for 4-24 hours.

3. Set the oven to preheat at 325°F with the wire rack in the middle of the oven.

4. Heat the oil in a large cast-iron pan over medium heat. When the oil is hot, brown the Turkey breast on both sides for approximately 4-5 minutes each.

5. Transfer the pan to the oven and cook for 1 hour and 30 minutes or until the breast is cooked through. Remove the pan from the oven and allow the turkey breast to rest for about 10 minutes.

6. Flip the breast to ensure that it has not stuck to the bottom of the pan. In a separate bowl. Whisk together the stock and flour until there are no lumps. Pour the stock into the pan and return the pan to the stove over medium heat, whisking continuously until the stock thickens.

7. Carve the turkey breast and serve with the sauce poured over the meat.

BEEF, LAMB & PORK

CHILI CON CARNE WITH A TWIST

COOK TIME: 1 HOUR 35 MINS | MAKES: 8 SERVINGS

INGREDIENTS:

- 2 tbsp. vegetable oil
- 4 tsp. crushed garlic
- 2 shallots, chopped
- 1 lb. ground beef
- 1 yellow bell pepper, seeded and sliced
- 1 red bell pepper, seeded and sliced
- 1/2 tsp. cinnamon
- 1/2 tsp. smoked paprika
- 1/4 tsp. red chili flakes
- 1/2 tsp. pepper
- 1 tsp. Himalayan salt

- 1 tbsp. dried oreganum
- 1/4 cup chili powder
- 1/4 cup chilies, seeded and chopped
- 2 bay leaves
- 2 tbsp. balsamic vinegar
- 2 tbsp. raw honey
- 3 cups turtle beans, rinsed and drained
- 2 cans crushed tomatoes
- 1 cup strong black coffee

DIRECTIONS:

1. In a large cast-iron pot, heat the oil over medium heat before adding the garlic and shallots. When the shallots are just starting to caramelize, add the ground beef, breaking it up with a wooden spoon as you stir. Mix in the peppers and cook until the beef is properly done and the peppers are soft. Stir in the spices and allow the meat to marinate for 5 minutes.

2. Add the rest of the ingredients and stir until the chili starts to boil. Lower the heat and allow the chili to simmer for 1 - 1 1/2 hours.

3. Remove the bay leaves before serving.

HACHIS PARMENTIER

COOK TIME: 1 HOUR 10 MINS | MAKES: 6 SERVINGS

INGREDIENTS:

- Himalayan salt
- 3 large potatoes, peeled and quartered
- 1 tsp. black pepper
- 1/2 cup tangy mayonnaise
- 1/2 cup melted butter
- 1 tsp. baking powder
- 2 tbsp. vegetable oil
- 4 tsp. crushed garlic

- 1 onion, diced
- 1 lb. ground beef
- 1 tsp. ground cumin
- 1 tbsp. mixed Italian herbs
- 1/4 tsp. cayenne pepper
- 2 large carrots, cubed
- 2 cups frozen peas

DIRECTIONS:

1. In a large cast-iron pot, cover the potatoes with generously salted water. Boil the potatoes for 15 minutes or until the potatoes are soft.

2. In a large bowl, beat the soft potatoes, 1 teaspoon of salt, pepper, mayonnaise, butter, and baking powder until the potatoes are light and fluffy. You can use an electric mixer to make the job easier.

3. In a cast-iron pan over medium heat, heat 1 tablespoon of the oil and add half of the garlic and all of the diced onion. When the onions are just beginning to caramelize, add the ground beef, cumin, Italian herbs, and cayenne pepper. Stir for 12 minutes or until the beef is properly cooked through. Pour the beef into a bowl and set aside for later.

4. Set the oven to preheat at 400°F.

5. In the same pan you used for the beef, heat 1 tablespoon of oil and add the garlic. When the garlic is soft, add the carrots and peas and cook until they are tender, after stirring for approximately 4 minutes, pour the vegetables into a separate bowl.

6. Pour the mince back into the pan and top with the vegetables. Use a wooden spoon to spread the mashed potatoes over the vegetables in an even layer, making sure that the mash touches the sides of the pan.

7. You can use a fork to draw patterns on the mash or bake in the oven as is, for 30 minutes or until the top is golden brown.

CHUNKY STIR-FRIED STEAK

COOK TIME: 20 MINS | MAKES: 4 SERVINGS

INGREDIENTS:

- 2 tsp. salt
- 1 tbsp. ground cumin
- 1 tbsp. dried oreganum
- 2 tsp. cayenne pepper
- 2 tsp. pepper
- 4 cube steaks
- 3 tbsp. olive oil

- 8 corn wraps
- 2 limes, halved
- 12 spring onions, chopped
- 8 cherry tomatoes, halved
- 2 yellow peppers, halved and seeded

DIRECTIONS:

1. Set the oven to preheat at 350°F. Place 2 large cast-iron pans on the stove and allow them to heat without any oil over medium-high heat.

2. In a small bowl, whisk together the salt, cumin, oreganum, cayenne pepper, and pepper. Use the spice mixture to massage the steaks until the spice has been distributed in an even layer over the steaks.

3. In your preheated pans, add 1 tablespoon of olive oil to each. With 2 steaks in each pan, brown the steaks on either side until they reach the required level of rarity. Approximately 10-12 minutes. Transfer the steaks to a platter and cover the platter with tin foil. Allowing the steaks to rest as you prepare the rest of the food.

4. Use tinfoil to cover the tortillas and allow them to heat in the oven while you prepare the vegetables.

5. Divide the remaining oil between the pans and turn up the heat. Toss all of the vegetables together with the limes in a bowl and divide them between the pans. Fry the vegetables until they are tender and the edges are just beginning to brown.

6. When everything is ready, reheat the steaks and squeeze the limes over the vegetables. Serve with the warmed wraps.

ROAST LAMB WITH RHUBARB RELISH

COOK TIME: 4 HOURS | MAKES: 8-10 SERVINGS

INGREDIENTS:

- 4 lamb shanks
- Himalayan salt
- 1 tbsp. fresh rosemary
- 1 cup garlic cloves, peeled
- 4 tbsp. olive oil
- 8 cups vegetable oil
- 1/4 cup white wine
- 8 rhubarb stalks, thinly sliced
- 1/2 cup brown sugar
- 1/4 cup balsamic vinegar
- 3 thyme sprigs
- 2 whole cloves
- black pepper
- 1 1/2 tbsp. French mustard
- 2 tbsp. lemon zest
- 2 tbsp. mint, chopped
- 2 tbsp. parsley, chopped
- 3 tbsp. horseradish, shredded

DIRECTIONS:

1. Set the oven to preheat at 250°F. Arrange the shanks on a baking sheet and use a generous amount of salt to massage each one. (About 1/2 teaspoon per shank.) Allow the shanks to chill in the fridge.

2. Meanwhile, place the rosemary, garlic, and 1/4 teaspoon of salt in a blender. Pulse to form a paste and gradually drizzle in 2 tablespoons of the olive oil. Once your paste is done, remove the lamb from the fridge and use your finger to rub the garlic paste into the shanks.

3. Transfer the shanks to a large cast-iron pot that is big enough to fit all four shanks. Pour the vegetable oil over the shanks before covering the pot with tin foil and baking in the oven for 2-3 hours until the lamb can easily be removed from the bone. Remove the pot from the oven and allow the shanks to rest on the counter.

4. In a small cast-iron pot over medium heat, stir together the white wine, rhubarb stalks, brown sugar, balsamic vinegar, thyme, and cloves. When the mixture begins to boil, lower the heat and simmer for 15 minutes until the relish begins to thicken. Remove the pot from the heat and use a slotted spoon to fish out the cloves and thyme. Season to taste with salt and pepper before mixing in the mustard.

5. Whisk together the lemon zest, mint, parsley, and shredded horseradish in a small bowl and set aside.

6. Set the oven to preheat at 350°F. Heat the remaining 2 tablespoons of olive oil in a pan over medium heat. Transfer the shanks from the pot into your pan with the heated oil. Brown the shanks in an even layer. About 8-10 minutes per side.

7. Place the browned shanks in an oven dish and heat them in the oven for approximately 10 minutes.

8. Once the shanks are properly heated. Arrange them on a platter. Use a basting brush to coat the shanks with your rhubarb relish and garnish with the mint and parsley mixture before serving.

SEARED PORK TENDERLOIN

COOK TIME: 30 MINS | MAKES: 4 SERVINGS

INGREDIENTS:

- 4 slices pork tenderloin
- black pepper
- coarse sea salt
- 1/2 cup all-purpose flour
- 4 tbsp. butter
- 2 tsp. garlic, minced
- 1 large onion, chopped
- 1 tbsp. crushed thyme

- 16 oz. Porcini mushrooms, cleaned and sliced
- 2 cups dry red wine
- cooked rice for serving

DIRECTIONS:

1. Place the tenderloin slices on a wooden chopping board and use a meat mallet to pound the pork. Sprinkle with a pinch of salt and pepper before coating the slices in a thick layer of flour.

2. Use a large cast-iron frying pan over medium heat to melt 2 tablespoons of butter. When the butter is hot, sear each slice of tenderloin, flipping after a few minutes. Once the pork is seared, place them on a platter and cover with tinfoil.

3. Return the pan to the heat and melt the remaining butter before caramelizing the garlic and onions. Stir in the thyme and mushrooms and cook until the mushrooms start to darken.

4. Whisk in the wine and allow the broth to simmer for 10 minutes.

5. Arrange the seared tenderloins on a bed of rice. Pour the sauce over the pork and serve.

SPICY GINGER BURGERS

COOK TIME: 20 MINS | MAKES: 4 SERVINGS

INGREDIENTS:

- 1/2 tsp. Himalayan salt
- 2 tbsp. hot sauce
- 1 tsp. ground ginger
- 2 tsp. crushed garlic
- 1 lb. ground beef
- 1 tbsp. vegetable oil
- 4 slices provolone cheese

- 1/4 tsp. ground ginger
- 1 tbsp. hot sauce
- 1/4 cup tangy mayonnaise
- 4 burger buns
- 1 cup iceberg lettuce, washed and rinsed
- 1 red onion, peeled and sliced

DIRECTIONS:

1. Using a wooden spoon in a medium bowl, mix together the salt, hot sauce, ginger, garlic, and ground beef until everything is properly combined. Roll the mixture into four evenly sized balls and flatten using a spatula to make the patties.

2. Using a cast-iron pan over medium heat, heat the oil. Arrange the patties in the pan and cook for 5-7 minutes before flipping. Place a slice of cheese on the cooked side of the patties while you fry the bottom. This will melt the cheese and seal in the flavor.

3. Meanwhile, whisk together the ginger, hot sauce, and tangy mayonnaise. Slice the buns and dollop a generous amount of sauce on the inside of each bun and use a knife to even it out.

4. Layer your buns with the lettuce and onion before placing a patty on each. Enjoy!

STUFFED BAVETTE STEAK

COOK TIME: 1 HOUR | MAKES: 4-6 SERVINGS

INGREDIENTS:

- 1 bavette steak (2 lb.)
- 2 tsp. steak spice
- 1/4 cup low sodium soy sauce
- 1/2 cup vegetable oil
- 4 tbsp. Butter
- 2 tbsp. crushed garlic
- 1/2 lb. provolone, thinly sliced

- 1/2 cup shallots, chopped
- 1/2 red bell pepper, seeded and sliced
- 1/2 cup porcini mushrooms, diced
- 1/2 cup spinach, Chopped
- 4 prosciutto slices

DIRECTIONS:

1. Arrange your bavette steak on a wooden chopping board with the broad end facing away from you. Starting from the top. Make slits horizontally across the meat, taking care to leave a 1/2" border on either side.

2. In a large bowl, whisk together the steak spice, soy sauce, and vegetable oil. Place your bavette steak in the bowl and toss to coat. Cover the bowl with tin foil and chill in the fridge for at least 4 hours before use.

3. Set the oven to preheat at 350°F. Use the butter to coat the inside of a large cast-iron pot.

4. Arrange your bavette steak on the length of a wooden chopping board. Dollop the garlic onto the steak and use a butter knife to fan it out. Season the garlic layer with a pinch of the steak spice. Arrange the cheese over the garlic in a single layer, leaving a small space around the edges so that cheese won't spill out.

5. Layer the shallots, bell pepper, mushrooms, spinach, and prosciutto over the cheese.

6. Starting at one end. Carefully roll up the meat as tight as you can without spilling any of the insides. Carefully lay the wheel on its side so that all the layers are visible. Use butcher's twine to secure the wheel in two or three sections.

7. Transfer the rolled bavette steak to your prepared pot and bake in the oven for 1 hour or until the steak is done to your liking.

8. Remove the pot from the oven and allow the steak to rest for 10 minutes before slicing and serving. You can use the twine as a guide to slice.

APPLE PICKLED PORK CHOPS

COOK TIME: 30 MINS | MAKES: 4 SERVINGS

INGREDIENTS:

- 2 tsp. whole cloves
- 1 bay leaf
- 1 tbsp. whole peppercorns
- 2 tbsp. coarse sea salt
- 4 cups apple cider
- 4 thick-cut pork chops
- olive oil
- 1 onion, chopped

- 3 green apples, peeled, cored, and sliced
- 1/4 cup apple cider
- 1/4 cup balsamic vinegar
- 1/3 tsp. crushed nutmeg
- 1 tbsp. brown sugar
- 1/4 tsp. Black pepper
- 1 tbsp. Dijon mustard

DIRECTIONS:

1. Use a medium cast-iron pot over medium heat, to mix the cloves, bay leaf, peppercorns, salt, and 1 cup of the cider. Bring the mixture to a boil and continue to stir until all the salt has dissolved. Stir in the remaining cups of cider. Remove the pot from the heat and allow the mixture to cool for about an hour. Add the pork chops to the pot and refrigerate for 12 hours.

2. Use a separate pot to heat 2 tablespoons of the olive oil and caramelize the onions before adding the apple slices. Cook until the apples are just beginning to brown.

3. Add 1/4 cup apple cider, balsamic vinegar, crushed nutmeg, sugar, and black pepper. Bring the mixture to a boil. Lower the heat and allow the mixture to simmer until the apples are soft. Remove the pot from the heat and stir in the mustard. Set aside.

4. Remove the chops from the marinade and allow the excess to drain on paper kitchen towels.

5. Heat 2 tablespoons of oil in a cast-iron frying pan and cook the chops for approximately 6 minutes before flipping and cooking the other side for an additional 6 minutes until the chops are properly done.

6. Serve the chops topped with the apple sauce.

CHORIZO & ENDIVE WITH BEANS

COOK TIME: 30 MINS | MAKES: 4-6 SERVINGS

INGREDIENTS:

- 1 lb. chorizo sausage
- 3 tbsp. olive oil
- 3 tsp. crushed garlic
- 1 can white kidney beans
- 1/2 tsp. cayenne pepper
- 1 bunch endive, cleaned and chopped
- 1/4 cup pecorino cheese, shredded

DIRECTIONS:

1. Place a cast-iron pan over medium heat to warm while you slice the sausage into 1/4-inch rounds. Once the pan is heated. Add the oil and the sausage rounds to the pan. When the sausage has heated through, add the garlic to the pan and stir. Mix in the can of beans with the juice, and the cayenne pepper. Reduce the heat and allow the mixture to simmer until most of the juice has cooked away.

2. Add the endive to the simmering pan and allow the leaves to cook for 5-7 minutes or until they start to soften and lose their crispness.

3. Plate and garnish with the cheese before serving.

SWEET & SPICY PORK TENDERLOIN

COOK TIME: 40 MINS | MAKES: 8-10 MINS

INGREDIENTS:

- 1/2 tsp. red pepper flakes
- 1/2 tsp. garlic powder
- 1/3 tsp. black pepper
- 1/2 tsp. ground cumin
- 1/2 tsp. chili powder
- 1/3 tsp. mustard powder
- 1/2 tsp. brown sugar
- 1/2 tsp. kosher salt

- 1 tsp. paprika
- 3 lb. pork tenderloin
- 1 tbsp. olive oil
- 14 oz. beef stock
- 2 cups heavy cream
- 3 tbsp. whole grain mustard

DIRECTIONS:

1. In a small glass bowl, whisk together all the spices and set aside. On a wooden cutting board, roughly chop the tenderloin into 2-inch squares. Transfer the meat into a medium bowl and use your hands to massage the spice mixture into the pork. Chill the meat for a minimum of 2 hours or up to 1 day.

2. Heat a large cast-iron pan over medium heat before adding the oil and pork. You want some room in the pan for the pork to fry, so you can do more than one batch if necessary. Once all of the beef is golden brown, mix in the stock. (If you have done more than one batch, add all the meat to the pan before adding the stock.

3. Allow the mixture to simmer for 15-20 minutes.

4. Meanwhile, in a small pot over medium heat, warm the cream. Whisk in the mustard.

5. Pour the mustard cream into your pan with the pork and simmer for an additional 10 minutes with the lid on or until your pork is properly cooked.

BACON HASLET WITH ONIONS

COOK TIME: 1 HOUR | MAKES: 4-6 SERVINGS

INGREDIENTS:

- 1/2 tsp. red pepper flakes
- 1 tsp. mustard powder
- 1 tsp. paprika
- 1 tsp. garlic powder
- 1 tsp. kosher salt
- 8 oz. cubed bacon, cooked (plus 2 tbsp. for garnish)
- 1 shallot, peeled and chopped
- 2 eggs

- 4 tsp. crushed garlic
- 1/2 cup full-cream milk
- 1/2 cup tomato paste
- 1 cup bread crumbs
- 2 lb. ground beef
- 1/2 cup tomato paste
- 3 tbsp. brown sugar
- 1/2 cup apple cider vinegar

DIRECTIONS:

1. Set the oven to preheat at 350°F.
2. Using a large bowl and a wooden spoon, combine the red pepper flakes, mustard powder, paprika, garlic powder, kosher salt, bacon, shallot, eggs, crushed garlic, milk, tomato paste, bread crumbs, and ground beef.
3. Lightly spray a cast-iron baking dish with cooking spray and press your beef mixture firmly into the dish.
4. In a separate bowl, beat the remaining tomato paste with the brown sugar and apple cider vinegar until you have a smooth paste.
5. Use a basting brush to coat your haslet with half of the paste before placing the dish in the oven for 1 hour.
6. Spread the rest of the paste over the haslet and serve with the extra bacon sprinkled on top.

MUSHROOM & KIDNEY PIE

COOK TIME: 2 HOURS | MAKES: 4 SERVINGS

INGREDIENTS:

- 1/2 lb. beef kidney
- 1/2 tsp. Himalayan salt
- 1/2 tsp. pepper
- 1/4 cup all-purpose flour
- 2 tbsp. olive oil
- 1 lb. beef, cubed
- 4 slices bacon, cubed

- 1 celery stalk, diced
- 1 shallot, chopped
- 4 0z. Porcini mushrooms, sliced
- 2 tsp. crushed garlic
- 1/2 cup red wine
- 12 oz. Guinness ale
- 1 thyme sprig

- 2 bay leaves
- 1 cup beef broth
- 17 oz. ready-made short crust pastry
- 1 egg yolk
- 2 tsp. cold water

DIRECTIONS:

1. Halve the kidney using a sharp knife and discard any excess skin or tubes. Chop the kidney into roughly 1-inch cubes. Use a large bowl to cover the kidney cubes with ice water and let them soak for 1 hour. Drain the kidney cubes and place them over two or more paper towels to soak up any excess water.
2. In a small bowl, whisk together the salt, pepper, and flour. Set aside.
3. Use a 12-inch cast-iron pan to heat the oil. You want the oil to be nice and hot but not so hot that it starts to smoke.
4. Combine the kidney and beef cubes in a large bowl, mix in the seasoned flour. Divide the meat into two batches as you don't want to overcrowd the pan. Seer the meat in the hot oil until it's nicely browned on all sides. Place the browned meat in a bowl and tent with foil.
5. Lower the heat in the pan and cook the bacon for a few minutes until it is nice and crispy. Add the celery and shallot, stirring for a few minutes until they start to brown. Toss in the mushrooms and garlic. When the mushrooms are beginning to darken, mix in the wine and ale. Allow the mixture to simmer until most of the liquid has evaporated.
6. Stir in the thyme, bay leaves, beef broth, and browned meat. Lower the heat to the minimum setting and place a lid on the pan. Allow the mixture to stew for 1 hour, or until the kidneys and beef are soft.
7. Discard the bay leaves and thyme sprig. Remove the pan from the heat. Once the mixture has cooled. Seal the pan with tin foil and chill for 6-12 hours.
8. Set the oven to preheat at 350°F.
9. On a lightly floured surface, roll out the pastry so that it is slightly bigger than the chilled pan of beef and kidneys. Carefully place the pastry lid over the pan and pinch the edges to seal.
10. In a small bowl, whisk together the egg yolk and water. Use a basting brush to coat the top of your pie. Place the pan in the oven for roughly 20-30 minutes or until the top is golden brown.
11. Serve straight away.

BACON & CHORIZO TOSSED RICE

COOK TIME: 1 HOUR 10 MINS | MAKES: 6-8 SERVINGS

INGREDIENTS:

- 8 baby potatoes
- 2 tbsp. olive oil
- 1/2 cup cipollini onions
- 8 Oz. bacon lardons (1/4-inch thick and 1-inch long)
- 3 whole cloves
- 1/2 cinnamon stick
- 1 shallot, diced
- 3 cups chicken broth
- 12 oz. spicy Italian sausage, diced

- 2 cups tomatoes, diced
- 1 bay leaf
- 1 1/2 cups basmati rice, rinsed
- 2 spring onions, chopped

DIRECTIONS:

1. Set the oven to preheat at 350°F.

2. In a large bowl, coat the potatoes with olive oil before arranging them on a baking pan. Place the pan in the oven for 10 minutes. Add the onions and return the pan to the oven for an additional 10 minutes or until a knife can easily slide in and out when inserted into the potatoes.

3. Allow the potatoes and onions to cool. Once they are cool, halve the potatoes. Peel the onions and chop them in half.

4. In a large cast-iron pot over medium heat, fry the bacon for about 8 minutes or until it is nice and crispy. Stir in the cloves and cinnamon, and allow them to fry until their fragrance is released. Add the shallots to the pan and stir continuously for approximately 6-8 minutes, or until the shallots begin to caramelize.

5. Stir in the cooked potatoes and garlic, along with the chicken broth, spicy Italian sausage, tomatoes, and bay leaf. Bring the mixture to a boil before gently stirring in the rice.

6. Cover the pot with tin foil and bake in the oven for 3o minutes. All of the liquid should be absorbed into the rice.

7. Plate and garnish with the spring onions before serving.

ZESTY ROASTED LAMB & POTATOES

COOK TIME: 2 HOURS | MAKES: 4 SERVINGS

INGREDIENTS:

- 1 leg of lamb (2 lb.)
- 3 garlic cloves, thinly sliced
- 1 tsp. kosher salt
- 1 lemon, juiced, and zested
- 2 tbsp. dried oregano
- 1/2 tsp. black pepper
- 2 tbsp. melted butter
- 1 cup boiling water

- 2 tbsp. olive oil
- 1 1/2 lb. baby potatoes, quartered
- pepper
- salt

DIRECTIONS:

1. Set the oven to preheat at 350°F, with the wire rack in the center of the oven.

2. Use a sharp knife to make small slits in the meat and insert the slices of garlic. In a small bowl, whisk together the salt, lemon juice, oregano, and pepper. Massage the mixture over the lamb in an even layer.

3. In a large cast-iron pan over medium heat, brown the lamb on all sides for approximately 4 minutes each. Transfer the lamb to a baking sheet. Place the sheet in the oven for 1 hour.

4. Discard any excess fat from the sheet. Use a basting brush to coat the lamb with the melted butter. Place the lamb back in the cast-iron pan. Pour the boiling water into the pan. Allow the lamb to cook for 45 minutes.

5. Use a large bowl to coat the potatoes in the oil and lemon zest. Season to taste with pepper and salt before arranging them around the lamb.

6. Place the pan in the oven for 45-60 minutes or until the lamb is falling off the bone and the potatoes are soft.

7. Remove the pan from the oven and cover with tin foil for 15 minutes before serving.

RIBS IN RED-WINE REDUCTION

COOK TIME: 2-3 HOURS | MAKES: 6 SERVINGS

INGREDIENTS:

- 5 lb. short ribs
- flaky seas salt
- black pepper
- 3 tbsp. olive oil
- 23 cups spring onions, diced
- 23 cups carrots, diced
- 23 cups shallots, diced
- 1 tbsp. crushed garlic
- 2 dried bay leaves

- 2 cups dry red wine
- 3/4 cups beef stock
- 1 3/4 cups water
- 1-2 tsp. red wine vinegar

DIRECTIONS:

1. Set the oven to preheat at 325°F with the wire rack in the middle of the oven.

2. Season the ribs to taste with salt and pepper. Set aside. Heat 2 tablespoons of oil over medium heat in a large cast-iron pot. When the oil is hot, brown the ribs on both sides, approximately 3-4 minutes per side. You can fry the ribs in 2 or 3 batches if they do not fit in the pot without overlapping. Set the ribs aside on a platter while you prepare the red-wine reduction.

3. Discard most of the fat from the pot before adding the remaining oil. When the oil is hot, add the spring onions, carrots, and shallots with a pinch of salt and pepper. Frying the vegetables until the shallots are just beginning to caramelize before stirring in the garlic and bay leaves. Stir for approximately 1 minute to release the flavor from the leaves.

4. Add 1/2 cup of the red wine to the pot and stir for approximately 1 minute, loosening any bits that may have stuck to the bottom. The wine should evaporate to about 2 tablespoons.

5. Mix in the remaining wine, beef stock, and water. Add the ribs along with all of the fat from the platter in two even layers. Cover the pot with foil and bake in the oven for 2-3 hours, turning the ribs every 40 minutes. It's okay if some of the meat falls off the bone, continue to cook until all of the meat is tender.

6. Remove the pot from the oven and arrange the ribs on a platter, leaving the sauce in the pot to cool for a few minutes. When the sauce has cooled, remove the fat from the surface before stirring in the vinegar.

7. Pour the sauce over the ribs and serve.

FISH & SEAFOOD

SEAFOOD WRAPS WITH MANGO SALAD

COOK TIME: 10 MINS | MAKES: 4 SERVINGS

INGREDIENTS:

- 2 tbsp. sunflower oil
- 3 tbsp. lime juice
- 2 tbsp. green chilies, seeded and diced
- 1 shallot, thinly sliced
- 1 cup mango, diced
- 1 1/2 cups purple cabbage, shredded
- 1 cup green cabbage, shredded
- Himalayan salt
- black pepper
- 2 tbsp. coriander leaves, finely chopped

- 2 tbsp. lime juice
- 2 avocados, chopped
- 1/4 cup sour cream
- 2 tbsp. lime juice
- 1/4 cup sunflower oil (plus 1 tbsp.)
- 1/2 tsp. cayenne pepper
- 1 tsp. crushed garlic
- 4 tilapia fillets
- 8 corn wraps

DIRECTIONS:

1. In a large bowl, stir together the oil, lime juice, chilis, shallot, mango, purple cabbage, and red cabbage until properly combined. Season to taste with salt and pepper. Chill for a maximum of 2 hours. Add the coriander right before building your wrap.

2. In a food processor, pulse the lime juice and avocado until properly combined before mixing in the sour cream. Transfer the avocado cream to a small bowl and sprinkle with a pinch of salt and pepper.

3. Use a medium bowl to whisk together 2 tablespoons lime juice, 1/4 cup sunflower oil, 1/2 teaspoon cayenne pepper, and 1 teaspoon garlic. Add the tilapia to the bowl, tossing to coat. Chill for 30-60 minutes.

4. Remove the tilapia from the sauce and shake off any extra sauce. Sprinkle the fish with a small amount of salt and pepper.

5. In a large cast-iron pan, heat the remaining tablespoon of oil. Once the oil is hot, fry the fish for approximately 4 minutes before flipping and frying the other side for an additional 5 minutes. If the fish sticks to the pan, it is not ready to be flipped.

6. Allow the fish to cool slightly before breaking the fish up with a fork.

7. Build your wraps by alternating between the fish, mango cabbage, and avocado cream. Don't forget to add the coriander leaves to the cabbage before serving.

SPICY LEMONGRASS MUSSELS

COOK TIME: 10-15 MINS | MAKES: 2 SERVINGS

INGREDIENTS:

- 1 bird's eye chili, chopped
- 1 piece of lemongrass, diced
- 1 yellow onion, chopped
- 2 tsp. crushed ginger
- 2 tsp. crushed garlic
- 1 tbsp. olive oil
- 1 tbsp. green curry paste
- 1 tbsp. fish sauce
- 15 oz. coconut milk
- 1 1/2-2 lb. mussels, beards removed and scrubbed

- cooked rice for serving
- coriander leaves, chopped
- 1 lime, juiced

DIRECTIONS:

1. Use a small cast-iron pot to whisk together the chili, lemongrass, onion, ginger, garlic, and olive oil over medium heat until the onions are tender.

2. Whisk in the curry paste and simmer for 30 seconds before stirring in the fish sauce and coconut milk. Add the mussels to the sauce, with the lid on the pot, cook the mussels for 5 minutes or until they open. Shaking the pot occasionally so that the mussels do not burn.

3. Serve the mussels over a bed of rice, throwing any away that have not opened while cooking.

4. Garnish with lime juice and coriander leaves. Enjoy!

BUTTERY SCALLOPS WITH TURNIP PUREE

COOK TIME: 20 MINS | MAKES: 4-6 SERVINGS

INGREDIENTS:

- 1/2 cup butter
- 1 lb. turnips, peeled and chopped (1-inch pieces)
- 2 thyme sprigs
- 2 tsp. garlic
- 1 bay leaf
- 1 cup heavy cream
- black pepper
- Himalayan salt
- 2 tbsp. olive oil
- 1 lb. scallops
- flaky sea salt

DIRECTIONS:

1. Heat the butter in a small cast-iron skillet until the milk separates and browns. Remove the skillet from the heat and set aside.

2. In a large cast-iron pot over medium heat, cover the turnips with water and boil for 10-12 minutes or until they are soft. Pour the turnips into a colander over the sink.

3. In a small cast-iron pot, heat the thyme, garlic, and bay leaf with the cream. Make sure it does not cool. You need it warm for the recipe.

4. In a food processor, pulse the drained turnips before gradually adding the warm cream while the machine is running. Season to taste with salt and pepper. Cover the puree so that it does not cool.

5. Use a cast-iron skillet over medium heat to heat the oil before adding the scallops. Brown the scallops on either side. About 1-2 minutes per side. Transfer the scallops to a platter. Pour the separated butter over the scallops before topping with the turnip puree. Garnish with a pinch of flaky sea salt.

THAI SPICED SHRIMP

COOK TIME: 5-10 MINS | MAKES: 3-4 SERVINGS

INGREDIENTS:

- 1/2 tsp. brown sugar
- 1 tsp. low sodium soy sauce
- 2 tbsp. water
- 2 tbsp. fish sauce
- 2 tbsp. olive oil
- 1 lb. shrimp
- 1 tbsp. crushed garlic

- 1 cup shallots, sliced
- 1 tsp. cayenne pepper
- 2 tbsp. coriander leaves, chopped
- 1/4 cup spring onions, chopped
- 3/4 cup basil leaves, torn into small pieces

DIRECTIONS:

1. Prepare and line up all of the ingredients before you begin so that they can be added in quick succession.

2. In a small glass bowl, whisk together the sugar, soy sauce, water, and fish sauce.

3. Heat a large cast-iron skillet over medium heat before adding the oil. Distribute the oil evenly over the skillet. In a single layer, fry the shrimp for a few seconds before flipping and frying for 15 seconds.

4. Toss in the garlic and shallots. Fry for 1 minute. The shallots should be soft but not browned.

5. Whisk the sauce once more before pouring it over the shrimp. Allow the shrimp to cook in the sauce without stirring for 1 minute.

6. Stir in the cayenne pepper, coriander leaves, and spring onions. Fry for 10seconds before adding the basil leaves and tossing.

7. Transfer to a bowl and serve.

SPICY ASIAN SALMON BURGERS

COOK TIME: 10-15 MINS | MAKES: 4 SERVINGS

INGREDIENTS:

- 1 tbsp. hot sauce
- 1/2 cup tangy mayonnaise
- 1/2 tsp. black pepper
- 1 tsp. salt
- 1/3 cup panko bread crumbs
- 2 tsp. ground ginger
- 6 spring onions, diced
- 2 tbsp. hoisin sauce
- 1/4 cup coriander leaves, chopped (extra for garnish)

- 1 1/2 lb. skinless salmon, cubed (1-inch pieces)
- 3 tbsp. toasted sesame oil
- 2 tbsp. Rice vinegar
- 1/2 cucumber, thinly sliced
- white pepper
- Himalayan salt
- 4 hamburger buns

DIRECTIONS:

1. Whisk together the hot sauce and mayonnaise in a small bowl and set aside.

2. In a blender, pulse 2 tablespoons of the mayonnaise mixture with the pepper, salt, bread crumbs, ginger, spring onions, hoisin sauce, coriander leaves, and salmon, leaving some chunks of salmon.

3. Form the mixture into 4, 1/2-inch patties. Place the patties in an airtight container and chill for 2-12 hours before frying.

4. In a medium bowl, mix together the sesame oil, rice vinegar, and cucumber. Season to taste with pepper and salt

5. Once the patties have chilled, heat a cast-iron broiler pan over medium-high heat and brown the patties, about 3-4 minutes per side. If you prefer a toasted bun you can set the patties aside to rest and scorch the buns on the hot broiler pan.

6. To build your burgers, slice the buns in half and dollop the mayonnaise and hot sauce on the inside of the buns, place the patties and top with your cucumber dressing. Garnish with the extra coriander leaves and serve!

FIERY FRIED GROUPER FILLETS

COOK TIME: 10 MINS | MAKES: 4 SERVINGS

INGREDIENTS:

- 1 tsp. ground black pepper
- 1 tsp. dried oreganum
- 1 tsp. flaky sea salt
- 1/4 tsp. chipotle powder
- 1/2 tsp. cayenne pepper
- 1/4 tsp. ground cumin
- 1 tsp. smoked paprika
- 4 grouper fillets, cleaned
- 4 tbsp. butter, melted
- 1 lemon, quartered

DIRECTIONS:

1. Whisk together all of the spices in a small bowl and set aside.

2. Place a large cast-iron pan over medium-high heat. While your pan is heating, use a basting brush to evenly coat the fish in the melted butter on both sides and season with the spice mixture.

3. Sear your fillets on both sides until darkened, 2-3 minutes per side.

4. Plate the fish and serve with the lemon quarters on the side. The fish is best when eaten with the lemon squeezed over the fillets.

HAZELNUT FRIED TROUT

COOK TIME: 10 MINS | MAKES: 2 SERVINGS

INGREDIENTS:

- 2 rainbow trout, cleaned
- 1/4 tsp. white pepper
- 1/2 tsp. Himalayan salt
- 1/2 cup flour
- 2 tbsp. butter
- 1/2 cup chopped hazelnuts
- 2 lemon slices

DIRECTIONS:

1. Rinse the fish with cool water and allow them to dry on paper kitchen towels.

2. In a large bowl, whisk together the pepper, salt, and flour. Dredge the fish in the flour and set aside.

3. Melt the butter in a large cast-iron pan over medium heat, tilt the pan so that the butter coats the bottom. Place the fish in the pan and fry for 5 minutes before flipping and adding the hazelnuts. Fry the fish on the other side for an additional 5 minutes. Toss the nuts frequently to avoid burning. The fish is done when the skin is browned and the fish is just beginning to break apart.

4. Plate the fish with the toasted nuts and serve with the lemon on top.

BLOOD ORANGE POACHED TUNA

COOK TIME: 10 MINS | MAKES: 4-6 SERVINGS

INGREDIENTS:

- 1/2 tsp. cayenne pepper
- 3 garlic cloves, skin on
- 3 thyme sprigs
- 3 rosemary sprigs
- 4 cups olive oil
- 3 blood oranges, peeled
- 4 celery sticks, chopped
- 2 tbsp. white wine vinegar
- 1/4 cup parsley, chopped
- Himalayan salt
- black pepper

DIRECTIONS:

1. Use a medium cast-iron pot to heat the cayenne pepper, garlic cloves, thyme, rosemary, and olive oil. The oil should be heated to just over 200°F when a candy thermometer is inserted.

2. Slice the blood oranges into a small bowl. Add the celery, vinegar, 3 tablespoons of the seasoned oil, and parsley. Sprinkle with salt and pepper to taste. Set aside.

3. Use a wire chip basket to carefully lower the fish into the oil and fry for 5-6 minutes or until the fish is golden brown, the inside should still be pink.

4. Plate the tuna and serve on a bed of the blood orange salad.

CRAB MEAT INDIENNE

COOK TIME: 10 MINS | MAKES: 4 SERVINGS

INGREDIENTS:

- 2 tbsp. butter
- 1 small shallot, chopped
- 2 tsp. curry powder
- 1 tsp. turmeric
- 3 tbsp. flour
- 2 cups chicken stock
- 1 1/2 cups crab meat
- cooked rice for serving

DIRECTIONS:

1. Melt the butter in a cast-iron pan over medium heat before adding the shallots and frying until they soften, about 3 minutes.

2. Whisk the curry powder, turmeric, and flour into the pan to form a thick paste. Whisk continuously for 2 minutes.

3. Gradually whisk in the chicken stock. Allow the mixture to simmer for 3 minutes while whisking to prevent lumps.

4. Finally stir in the crab meat until it's heated through. Serve on a bed of cooked rice.

SAUTÉED SEA BASS FILLETS

COOK TIME: 10 MINS | MAKES: 4 SERVINGS

INGREDIENTS:

- flaky sea salt
- ground peppercorns
- 4 sea bass fillets
- 1/4 cup vegetable oil
- 1/2 cup lemon juice
- 1/4 cup fresh basil, chopped
- 1/2 cup toasted pine nuts
- 1/4 cup parsley

DIRECTIONS:

1. Heat 2 tablespoons of oil in a cast-iron pan over medium heat. While the oil is heating, season your filets on both sides with a generous pinch of salt and pepper.

2. Once the oil is ready, brown the fish for 2 minutes or until the edges are solid. Flip and fry for an additional 2 minutes. You can do 2 or 3 batches if necessary, don't overcrowd the pan. Set the cooked filets aside on a warmed plate.

3. Add the lemon juice to the pan and simmer until most of the juice has evaporated and about 3 table-spoons remain. Carefully loosen any bits that may have stuck to the bottom of the pan.

4. Stir in the basil and pine nuts before removing the pan from the heat and dolloping the sauce over your filets. Garnish with parsley and serve.

SPICY SHRIMP IN GARLIC SAUCE

COOK TIME: 15 MINS | MAKES: 4 SERVINGS

INGREDIENTS:

- 1 tbsp. low sodium soy sauce
- 1 tbsp. fish sauce
- 3 tsp. crushed garlic
- 3 tbsp. chili paste
- 1/2 tsp. kosher salt
- 1 lb. shrimp, peeled and deveined
- 2 tbsp. butter
- 1 tbsp. olive oil
- 2 tbsp. coriander leaves, chopped
- 1/2 lime, juiced

DIRECTIONS:

1. Use a medium bowl to whisk together the soy sauce, fish sauce, garlic, chili paste, and salt before adding the shrimp and tossing to coat.

2. In a large cast-iron pan over medium heat, melt the butter and stir in the oil.

3. Pour the shrimp, along with all the sauce into your pan and fry until the shrimp blush (Turn a light shade of pink) and curl into a C.

4. Transfer the shrimp and sauce to a platter. Garnish with the coriander leaves and lime juice before serving.

SOLE IN GARLIC & VERMOUTH

COOK TIME: 20 MINS | MAKES: 4 SERVINGS

INGREDIENTS:

- 4 tbsp. butter
- 4 garlic cloves, chopped
- 10 oz. button mushrooms, cleaned and sliced
- 1/4 tsp. white pepper
- 1/2 tsp. sea salt
- 1 tbsp. red wine vinegar
- 3 1/2 tbsp. parsley, chopped (extra for garnish)
- 1/2 cup dry vermouth
- 4 sole fillets, skinned and cleaned

DIRECTIONS:

1. Melt 3 tablespoons of butter in a large cast-iron pan over medium-high heat. When the butter is melted, add the garlic and cook for 45 seconds, tossing occasionally. Stir in the mushrooms for about 5-7 minutes or until they have darkened.

2. Season the mushrooms with pepper and salt before stirring in the vinegar, parsley, and vermouth. Boil the sauce for about 2 minutes until most of the liquid has evaporated, about half.

3. Transfer the pan to a wooden chopping board or potholder. Submerge the fish in the pan, carefully sloshing the sauce over the fillets, and place a lid on the pan.

4. Reduce the heat on the stove and simmer the fish for 7-12 minutes or until the fish is almost cooked through.

5. Transfer the fillets to a warmed plate. Leave the sauce on the stove and whisk in the remaining butter.

6. Pour the sauce over the fish and garnish with the extra parsley before serving.

BREAD & PASTA

PAN-FRIED CORN-PONE

COOK TIME: 22-25 MINS | MAKES: 4 SERVINGS

INGREDIENTS:

- 4 tbsp. butter, melted, extra for greasing the pan
- 1/2 tsp. Himalayan salt
- 1/2 tsp. bicarbonate of soda
- 1/2 tsp. baking powder
- 1 cup corn flour
- 1 cup all-purpose flour
- 1 large egg
- 1 cup buttermilk
- 2 tbsp. raw honey

DIRECTIONS:

1. Coat an 8-inch cast-iron pan with butter and set the oven to preheat at 400°F.
2. Using a medium bowl, whisk together the salt, bicarb, baking powder, corn flour, and salt.
3. Use a separate bowl to whisk together the melted butter, egg, buttermilk, and honey to form a slightly lumpy mixture.
4. Pour the mixture into the bowl with the flour and use a wooden spoon to combine the ingredients.
5. Transfer your batter to the greased pan and bake in the oven for 22-25 minutes or until an inserted skewer comes out dry and the top is golden brown.
6. Allow the corn-pone to cool slightly before slicing and serving.

EASY DINNER ROLLS

COOK TIME: 12-15 MINS | MAKES: 14 ROLLS

INGREDIENTS:

- 1/4 oz. active dry yeast
- 1/2 cup warm water
- 1/2 tsp. bicarbonate of soda
- 2 tsp. baking powder
- 2 tsp. brown sugar
- 1 teaspoon kosher salt
- 3 cups all-purpose flour (more if needed)

- 1 cup buttermilk
- 2 tbsp. vegetable fat, melted

DIRECTIONS:

1. Butter a large cast-iron pan and set aside.

2. Whisk the yeast into the warm water and allow the mixture to bloom on the counter for a few minutes.

3. In a large bowl, whisk together the bicarb, baking powder, sugar, salt, and flour.

4. Using a wooden spoon, mix in the bloomed yeast, buttermilk, and vegetable fat until properly combined. (You may add more flour at this point if you prefer denser rolls.)

5. Sprinkle your counter with flour before turning out the dough and working it for a few minutes until it's dry to the touch. Shape your dough into a rectangle and use a very sharp knife to slice 14 rolls. It is important that your knife is sharp and you cut directly down as this will determine how well they rise.

6. Arrange your rolls in the buttered pan and cover them with greaseproof paper. Allow the rolls to rise for 1 hour in a warm, draft-free area or until they have doubled in size.

7. In an oven that has been preheated to 425°F, bake the rolls for 12-15 minutes or until they are golden brown.

8. The rolls are best served straight away with butter.

CRISPY ITALIAN PAN BREAD

COOK TIME: 25 MINS: | MAKES: 4-6 SERVINGS

INGREDIENTS:

- 1/2 tsp. Himalayan salt
- 6 tbsp. extra virgin olive oil, divided
- 1 tbsp. active dry yeast
- 1 cup warm water
- 2 1/2 cups all-purpose flour
- 1 tbsp. crushed rosemary

- 3 tsp. crushed garlic
- flaky sea salt
- black pepper

DIRECTIONS:

1. Use a crumpled-up piece of greaseproof paper to coat a large bowl in olive oil.

2. In a separate bowl, whisk together the salt, 3 tablespoons of olive oil, yeast, and warm water. Allow the mixture to bloom for about 10 minutes on the counter.

3. Use a wooden spoon to gradually mix the flour into your bloomed yeast.

4. Once your dough has just come together, lightly flour a counter and work the dough for 10-12 minutes or until it is smooth and elastic.

5. Place your dough in the bowl with olive oil, turning to lightly grease the dough. Use a slightly damp tea towel to cover the bowl and allow the dough to rise in a warm, draft-free area until the dough has expanded, about 1 hour.

6. Use a basting brush to lightly grease a cast-iron pan with 2 tablespoons of olive oil. Knead your dough into a rough ball and place it in the middle of the pan. Cover and allow to expand once more for 45 minutes.

7. Set the oven to preheat at 400°F.

8. In a small glass bowl, whisk together the remaining olive oil, garlic, rosemary, and a pinch of sea salt and black pepper. Use your finger to create tiny pockets in the dough before brushing the olive oil and garlic mixture over the bread.

9. Place the pan in the oven and bake for 25 minutes or until the bread is nicely crusted on top.

10. Let the bread cool in the pan for a few minutes before slicing.

SIMPLE POT BREAD

COOK TIME: 1 HOUR | MAKES: 4 SERVINGS

INGREDIENTS:

- 1/4 tsp. active dry yeast
- 2 tsp. sea salt
- 3 cups brown bread flour (extra for dusting)
- 1 1/3 cup warm water (more if needed)
- 3 tbsp. butter, melted (optional)

DIRECTIONS:

1. Whisk together all of the dry ingredients in a large bowl, gradually stir in the water until everything is properly combined. If the dough is too dry, add more water a little at a time. You want a sticky mixture. Cover the bowl with a slightly damp tea towel and allow the dough to rise in a warm area for 18-24 hours or until the dough has doubled in size.

2. Turn your dough out onto a lightly floured counter. Gently bring all of the dough together in a ball and fold the sides of the dough under the ball, exposing the middle. Place your dough in between a sheet of greaseproof paper and a tea towel. Allow the dough to once again double in size for about 1-2 hours.

3. Set the oven to preheat at 475°F with a medium cast-iron pot in the middle of the oven.

4. Once the pot has been in the oven for a few minutes and is nice and hot, carefully lower your dough into the pot, with the greaseproof paper at the bottom. Place the lid on the pot and bake for 30 minutes. Remove the lid and bake for an additional 20-30 minutes or until the bread has a lovely golden crust.

5. Turn the bread out onto a wire rack and cool for about 1 hour before serving.

6. You can brush the melted butter over the top of the bread while it is cooling for a buttery flavor if desired.

ONE-PAN CHEESY LASAGNA

COOK TIME: 25-30 MINS | MAKES: 12 SERVINGS

INGREDIENTS:

- 1 tbsp. olive oil
- 1 shallot, diced
- 4 tsp. crushed garlic
- 1/2 lb. Italian sausage
- 1/2 lb. ground beef
- kosher salt
- black pepper
- 1/4 tsp. crushed rosemary
- 1/4 tsp. crushed basil
- 1 tsp. white pepper

- 1/2 tsp. oregano
- 1/2 tsp. thyme
- 1 tsp. raw honey
- 1 can diced tomatoes (14 1/2 oz.)
- 15 oz. tomato puree
- 8 0z. lasagna sheets, broken into pieces
- 1/4 cup parmesan, grated
- 3/4 cups cream cheese
- 8 oz. mozzarella, thinly sliced
- 1/4 cup fresh basil leaves

DIRECTIONS:

1. Use a large cast-iron pan to heat the olive oil over medium-high heat. Add the shallots and garlic to the pan, fry for a few minutes until the shallots just begin to caramelize. Stir in the beef and mix until properly browned, season to taste with a pinch of salt and pepper. Place the pan on a wooden chopping board while you prepare the rest of the dish.

2. Lower the heat on the stove to medium. In a separate cast-iron pan, stir together the rosemary, basil, pepper, oregano, thyme, honey, tomatoes with the juice, and tomato puree. Stir until the mixture starts to simmer.

3. Stir in the broken lasagna sheets and allow them to cook for about 12 minutes or until they are al dente. Stirring throughout to prevent burning. Combine the contents of the two pans into one.

4. Preheat the broiler in your oven.

5. Mix the cream cheese and parmesan before creating little pockets in your pan of meat and sauce. Spoon the cheese mixture into your sauce and cover with the meat.

6. Layer the mozzarella on top of the sauce and broil the pan in the oven for a few minutes until the cheese is melted and bubbly.

7. Serve with the basil leaves sprinkled on top.

SHRIMP PASTA IN TIPSY SAUCE

COOK TIME: 5-10 MINS | MAKES: 8 SERVINGS

INGREDIENTS:

- 1/2 tsp. cayenne pepper
- 1/4 tsp. white pepper
- 1 tsp. sea salt
- 28 oz. chopped, canned tomatoes
- 1 Sharwil avocado, peeled and chopped
- 3 tbsp. cold butter
- 1/2 cup tequila
- 1 1/2 lb. shrimp, cleaned and deveined

- 1 lb. ribbon pasta cooked for serving
- 1/4 cup coriander leaves, chopped

DIRECTIONS:

1. In a food processor, combine the cayenne pepper, white pepper, sea salt, tomatoes, and half of the avocado, processing until just combined. You don't want a completely smooth mixture.

2. Melt half of the butter in a cast-iron pan over medium heat. When the butter is bubbling, stir in the tequila and shrimp. Stir continuously for 2 minutes until the shrimp blush and curl into a C. Most of the tequila should have evaporated at this stage.

3. Stir in the remaining butter and processed avocado mixture.

4. Pour the shrimp and sauce over your cooked pasta. Sprinkle the coriander leaves and remaining avocado over the dish before serving.

BROILED CHEDDAR MACARONI

COOK TIME: 15-20 MINS | MAKES: 4 SERVINGS

INGREDIENTS:

- 2 tbsp. olive oil
- sea salt
- 12 oz. elbow macaroni
- 3 tbsp. butter
- 3 tbsp. all-purpose flour
- 2 cups full-cream milk
- 1/2 tsp. crushed thyme
- 1 tbsp. Worcestershire sauce
- 1 tbsp. French mustard

- 14 oz. cheddar cheese, shredded
- 14 oz. Swiss cheese, shredded
- black pepper
- Himalayan salt
- 3 cups parmesan cheese, shredded

DIRECTIONS:

1. Preheat the broiler to high and place a wire rack about 4-inches away from the broiler.

2. Place your elbow macaroni in a large saucepan and cover with salty water and 2 tablespoons of olive oil, remember when you are making pasta, you want the water to be salty like the sea. The olive oil will prevent the pasta from sticking together. Boil the macaroni until it is al dente. Use a colander to drain the pasta and set aside.

3. In a 12-inch cast-iron pan over medium heat, melt the butter before whisking in the flour to form a paste. Gradually pour in the milk, whisking continuously. The sauce should begin to thicken after about 2 minutes.

4. Whisk in the thyme, Worcestershire sauce, cheddar, and Swiss cheese until all the cheese has melted into the sauce. Remove the saucepan from the plate and season to taste with pepper and salt.

5. Add the pasta to the sauce and mix until all the macaroni is completely immersed in the sauce. Sprinkle the parmesan in an even layer over the pasta and sauce. Place the pan under the broiler for 3-4 minutes or until your macaroni is bubbling.

6. Serve immediately.

SHREDDED PORK PASTA SAUCE

COOK TIME: 2 HOURS | MAKES: 6-8 SERVINGS

INGREDIENTS:

- 1 tbsp. olive oil
- kosher salt
- black pepper
- 2 lb. boneless pork shoulder
- 2 cups shallots, finely chopped
- 3 tsp. crushed garlic
- 1 cup dry red wine

- 3 dried bay leaves
- 3 cups tomato purée
- 1/2 lb. sweet Italian sausage

DIRECTIONS:

1. In a large cast-iron pot, heat the oil over medium-high heat until it just begins to simmer. Generously season the pork with salt and pepper before placing it in the pot and browning each side, approximately 3-4 minutes per side. Leave the pork to rest on a plate while you prepare the rest of the dish.

2. Add the shallots and garlic to the pot, lower the heat to medium-low and stir for 7-8 minutes or until the shallots are tender and just beginning to caramelize. Add the pork back to the pot and cover with the wine. Turn the stove back up to medium-high and allow the wine to simmer for a minute or two before stirring in the bay leaves and tomato purée. Once the sauce has begun to boil, reduce the heat and simmer with the lid on while you prepare the sausage.

3. Prepare the sausages by removing the meat from the skin and breaking it into chunks. Add the sausage chunks to the pot and simmer for 30 minutes with the lid on. Keep an eye on the heat so that the sauce does not begin to boil again.

4. After 30 minutes, turn the meat and continue to simmer for an additional hour or until all of the pork is tender. You can turn the meat a few times throughout the simmering process.

5. Once your pork is tender, carefully remove the meat from the pot with a slotted spoon or tongs. Use a knife and fork to shred the meat, you may also wait a few minutes for it to cool slightly, making it easier to work with.

6. Add the shredded pork to the pot and stir. Serve immediately over pasta or keep in the freezer for 3 months and up to 3 days in the fridge using a sealed container.

SKILLET CAVATELLI

COOK TIME: 15-20 MINS | MAKES: 4-6 SERVINGS

INGREDIENTS:

- 1 lb. cavatelli dry pasta
- sea salt
- 3 tbsp. olive oil
- 1 lb. chicken sausage
- 1/4 cup chicken broth
- 3/4 lb. spinach, cleaned and roughly chopped

- 1 tsp. lemon zest
- 1/3 tsp. cayenne pepper
- 1/2 cup parmesan, shredded
- kosher salt
- black pepper

DIRECTIONS:

1. Place the cavatelli in a large cast-iron pot and cover the pasta with salty water and 1 tablespoon of olive oil. Bring the pasta to a boil and cook until it reaches the desired softness. Strain in a colander and set aside.

2. Return the cast-iron pot to the stove and heat the remaining olive oil. Prepare the chicken sausage by removing the meat from the casings and breaking it up into small chunks. Add the broken-up sausage to the pot and brown for 5-7 minutes. The sausage will gradually break apart as you stir.

3. Mix in the chicken broth and spinach, allowing it to cook for 3-4 minutes or until the spinach has reduced.

4. Add the pasta to the pot along with the lemon zest, cayenne pepper, and parmesan. Stir until everything is properly combined. If there is too much sauce, you can leave the pot on the heat for a few more minutes until the sauce reduces.

5. Season to taste with salt and pepper before serving.

SKILLET STROGANOV

COOK TIME: 1-2 HOURS | MAKES: 4 SERVINGS

INGREDIENTS:

- 1 tbsp. olive oil
- 1 lb. beef, cubed (1-inch thick cubes)
- 2 tsp. crushed garlic
- 1 shallot, chopped
- 1/4 lb. porcini mushrooms, sliced
- 1/2 cup sherry
- 1 1/2 cups beef stock
- 1 bay leaf, torn in half
- 1/4 tsp. crushed thyme

- 1/4 tsp. white pepper
- 1/4 tsp. salt
- 1/2 tsp. crushed oregano
- 2 tbsp. water
- 1/4 cup all-purpose flour
- 1/2 cup sour cream
- cooked pasta for serving

DIRECTIONS:

1. Set the oven to preheat at 325°F with the wire rack in the middle of the oven.

2. Heat a cast-iron pan over medium heat before adding the olive oil. When the oil is hot, brown the beef cubes. Discard any excess fat from the pan.

3. Stir in the garlic, shallots, and mushrooms, cook for 5-7 minutes or until the mushrooms darken and shallots just begin to caramelize. Stir in the sherry, beef stock, bay leaf halves, thyme, pepper, salt, and oregano. Place the pan in the oven and bake for 1 1/2 hours. Remove the pan from the oven after 1 1/2 hours, take out the bay leaf halves and transfer the beef to a warmed plate and cover with tin foil.

4. Heat the pan with the sauce over low heat. Meanwhile, whisk together the water, flour, and sour cream in a small bowl. Carefully remove a cup of the sauce from the pan and gradually whisk it into your sour cream mixture until everything is properly combined.

5. Once you have a lump-free mixture, gradually whisk it into the pan. Stir in the beef that was set aside and allow the meat to marinate in the sauce for an extra 3 minutes over the heat.

6. Serve the Stroganov on a bed of pasta.

SPICY SHRIMP LINGUINI

COOK TIME: 10-15 MINS | MAKES: 5-6 SERVINGS

INGREDIENTS:

- 3 tbsp. olive oil
- 1 lb. shrimp, shelled and deveined
- 1 tsp. Himalayan salt
- 1 tsp. cayenne pepper
- 1/4 cup Riesling wine
- 4 tsp. garlic cloves, sliced

- 1 tsp. red pepper flakes
- 1 cup dry white wine
- 15 oz. tomatoes, chopped
- 1/4 cup parsley, chopped
- cooked linguini for serving
- parmesan, grated

DIRECTIONS:

1. Heat a cast-iron pan over medium heat. Add 1 tablespoon of oil, shrimp, salt, and cayenne pepper, stirring continuously for 2 minutes.

2. Remove the pan from the heat and gently stir in the Riesling wine. Set aside for 2 minutes or until most of the wine has reduced. Transfer to a bowl, scraping out all the sauce with a wooden spoon.

3. Heat the pan again before adding the remaining oil and garlic. Once the garlic has browned, add the red pepper flakes, dry white wine, and tomatoes to the pan, stirring until everything is combined. Allow the mixture to simmer for about 10 minutes before stirring in the parsley.

4. Serve the shrimp on a bed of Linguini and top with the sauce and parmesan.

CHARD & RICOTTA STUFFED SHELLS

COOK TIME: 35-40 MINS | MAKES: 4-6 SERVINGS

INGREDIENTS:

- 2 cups mozzarella cheese, shredded
- 1 cup parmesan cheese, shredded
- 15 oz. ricotta cheese
- 1 large egg
- 1/4 cup fresh basil, chopped
- 2 tbsp. fresh parsley, chopped (extra for garnish)
- 1/4 tsp. crushed nutmeg
- 1/4 tsp. cayenne pepper
- Himalayan salt

- 3 tbsp. olive oil
- 5 oz. chard, chopped
- 1 shallot, diced
- 3 tsp. crushed garlic
- 28 oz. canned tomatoes
- 2 tsp. Worcestershire sauce
- black pepper
- 8 oz. large pasta shells, cooked

DIRECTIONS:

1. Set the oven to preheat at 325°F.

2. Using a wooden spoon in a large bowl, mix together half of the mozzarella and half of the parmesan. Add the ricotta cheese, egg, basil, parsley, nutmeg, cayenne pepper, and a pinch of salt, stirring until everything is properly combined.

3. Heat a large cast-iron skillet over medium heat and add 1 tablespoon of olive oil. Once the oil is hot, stir in the chard and cook until it has reduced. Transfer the cooked chard to a bowl lined with paper towels and drain most of the water. Stir the drained chard into your bowl of ricotta.

4. Return the skillet to the stove and heat the remaining oil. Add the shallots to the skillet and caramelize. Stir in the garlic for 30 seconds before adding the tomatoes along with their juices and the Worcestershire sauce. Stir until the sauce begins to thicken, about 5 minutes. Season to taste with salt and pepper.

5. Stuff the large cooked pasta shells with the ricotta and chard. Arrange them face up in the pan of sauce, using a ladle, spoon some of the sauce over the stuffed shells. Sprinkle the remaining parmesan and mozzarella over the shells.

6. Use tin foil to cover the pan and bake in the oven for 25 minutes. Remove the pan from the oven and discard the foil. Bake for an additional 10 minutes or until the cheese is bubbling and nicely browned. Garnish with parsley and serve straight away.

SOUPS & STEWS

HEARTY ITALIAN BEEF STEW

COOK TIME: 25-30 MINS | MAKES: 6-8 SERVINGS

INGREDIENTS:

- 2 tbsp. olive oil
- 1 shallot, chopped
- 1 lb. ground beef
- 3 cups water
- 1 tsp. ground cumin
- 1/2 cup zesty Italian dressing
- 14 1/2 oz. beef stock

- 1 1/2 cups frozen corn, thawed and drained
- 15 oz. turtle beans, drained
- 28 oz. crushed tomatoes
- 1 cup bowtie pasta
- 1 cup marble jack cheese, grated

DIRECTIONS:

1. Heat the olive oil in a large cast-iron pot over medium heat. When the oil is hot, add the shallots and stir for a few minutes until they begin to caramelize. Add the beef and cook until it is nicely browned. Discard any excess fat and oil from the pan.

2. Stir in the water, cumin, Italian dressing, beef stock, corn, turtle beans, and crushed tomatoes. Bring the mixture to a boil before adding the pasta and cooking for about 8 minutes or until the pasta is al dente.

3. Spoon the stew into bowls and serve with a sprinkling of cheese on top.

ASIAN BUTTERNUT & YAM SOUP

COOK TIME: 30 MINS | MAKES: 6-8 SERVINGS

INGREDIENTS:

- 1/2 cup water
- 1 tbsp. lemon juice
- 1 cup white sugar
- 2 tbsp. butter.
- 1/2 cup toasted black sesame seeds
- flaky seas salt
- 3 lb. butternut, peeled, seeded, and cubed
- 4 tbsp. olive oil
- kosher salt
- black pepper
- 1 lb. yams, peeled and diced
- 1 shallot, diced
- 2 tsp. crushed garlic
- 1/3 tsp. crushed nutmeg
- 4 cups vegetable broth
- 2 tbsp. yellow miso
- 4 tbsp. sour cream

DIRECTIONS:

1. In a small cast-iron pot over medium heat, stir together the water, lemon juice, and sugar until all the granules have dissolved and the mixture starts to darken about 8 minutes. Stir in the butter before adding the sesame seeds. Pour the melted sugar onto a cookie pan lined with greaseproof paper. Sprinkle the salt over the melted sugar and allow it to harden on the counter. Once the sugar has hardened, use a wooden mallet to break it into small pieces.

2. Line a baking sheet with greaseproof paper and set the oven to preheat at 425°F.

3. Toss the butternut cubes in a bowl with 2 tablespoons of olive oil and a pinch of salt and pepper. Fan the butternut out on the cookie sheet and bake in the oven for 30-40 minutes or until the cubes are fork-tender. Allow the butternut to cool while you prepare the rest of the dish.

4. Over medium heat in a large cast-iron pot, heat the remaining olive oil and add the yams and shallot. Cook until the yams are tender, about 10-12 minutes. Stir in the garlic and nutmeg for 30 seconds. Add the cooked pumpkin and stir for an additional 5 minutes before adding the vegetable stock and miso. Once the soup is boiling, lower the heat and simmer uncovered for 5 minutes.

5. Use a hand held blender to puree the soup, mix in the sour cream and in bowls with the melted sesame sugar for garnish.

CHEESY BROCCOLI SOUP

COOK TIME: 20 MINS | MAKES: 6-8 SERVINGS

INGREDIENTS:

- 1 lb. broccoli, cored
- sea salt
- 2 tbsp. butter
- 1 shallot diced
- 1 tsp. crushed garlic
- 1/3 tsp. red pepper flakes
- 1/2 tsp. crushed nutmeg

- 2 tbsp. all-purpose flour
- 2 cups water
- 2 cups chicken stock
- 3 thyme sprigs
- 1/2 cup heavy cream
- 4 cups cheddar cheese, shredded
- black pepper

DIRECTIONS:

1. Separate the broccoli into 1-inch florets. Bring them to a boil in a large cast-iron pot of salted water. Once the broccoli is soft, drain in a colander and set aside.

2. In a large cast-iron pot over medium heat, melt the butter before adding the shallots and a pinch of salt. Cook the shallots for about 10-12 minutes until they start to caramelize. Stir in the garlic.

3. Whisk in the red pepper flakes, nutmeg, and flour, allowing the paste to cook for 3 minutes. Whisking throughout.

4. Stir in the water, stock, cream, and thyme. Once the soup is boiling, stir in the cheese until all of it has melted. Let the soup simmer for an additional 5 minutes before adding the broccoli.

5. Use a handheld blender to purée the soup. Season to taste with salt and pepper.

6. Serve straight away.

SPICY CHICKEN & COCONUT SOUP

COOK TIME: 20 MINS | MAKES: 2 SERVINGS

INGREDIENTS:

- 1 lemongrass stalk, peeled
- 15 Oz. chicken stock
- 15 oz. coconut milk
- 2 limes, zested
- 1 tsp. crushed ginger
- 2 tsp. red pepper flakes
- 1 tsp. raw honey
- 3 limes, juiced
- 1/2 cup fish sauce

- 4 oz. porcini mushrooms, diced
- 1/2 lb. chicken breasts, cubed
- kosher salt
- black pepper
- 1/2 cup coriander leaves, chopped

DIRECTIONS:

1. Trim the ends of the lemongrass and dice the stalk into 1-inch cubes.

2. In a large cast-iron pot over medium heat, whisk together the lemongrass, chicken stock, coconut milk, lime zest, and ginger. Bring to a boil while covered.

3. Stir in the pepper flakes, honey, lime juice, fish sauce, mushrooms, and cubed chicken. Boil the soup until the chicken is properly cooked and the mushrooms are soft. Season to taste with salt and pepper.

4. Discard the lemongrass. Ladle the soup into bowls and garnish with the coriander leaves before serving.

CLAM & POTATO SOUP

COOK TIME: 30 MINS | MAKES: 5 SERVINGS

INGREDIENTS:

- 1 tbsp. olive oil
- 2 slices thick-cut bacon, cubed (1/4" cubes)
- 1 shallot, chopped
- 1 bay leaf, torn in half
- 3 celery stalks, chopped
- 1 tsp. Himalayan salt
- 1/2 tsp. crushed thyme
- 1/2 cup white wine
- 2 medium potatoes, peeled and cubed (1/3" cubes)

- 16 1/2 oz. canned clams, chopped
- 2 cups full-cream milk
- 1/4 cup parsley, chopped (extra for garnish)
- white pepper

DIRECTIONS:

1. Heat the olive oil in a large cast-iron pot over medium heat. When the oil is hot, fry the bacon cubes for 3-4 minutes or until the edges are nice and crispy. Carefully transfer the bacon to a bowl that has been lined with paper towels and set aside.

2. With the oil and all of the fat from the bacon still in the pot, stir in the shallots, bay leaf halves, celery, 1/2 teaspoon of salt, and thyme. Place the lid on the pot and allow the vegetables to cook for about 4 minutes or until the vegetables are fork-tender. You can stir the pot a few times to prevent the vegetables from burning.

3. Add the wine and allow the vegetables to marinate with the lid off the pot until the wine has mostly evaporated, about 2 minutes.

4. Stir in the potatoes, sauce from the canned clams, and milk. Allow the soup to simmer for 8-10 minutes or until the potatoes are tender.

5. Use a handheld blender to puree the contents of the pot before adding the parsley, and clams. Season with the remaining salt and a pinch of pepper.

6. Pour the soup into bowls and sprinkle with the bacon and extra parsley before serving.

HEARTY ITALIAN EGG DROP SOUP

COOK TIME: 15-20 MINS | MAKES: 4 SERVINGS

INGREDIENTS:

- 6 cups chicken stock
- 1 1/2 tsp. kosher salt
- 1/3 tsp. nutmeg
- 1 tbsp. parsley, chopped
- 2 tsp. crushed garlic
- 1/3 cup parmesan, shredded
- 4 large eggs
- 12 oz. ground pork
- 4 tbsp. plain bread crumbs
- 10 oz. cream cheese

DIRECTIONS:

1. Bring the chicken stock to a boil in a large cast-iron pot over medium heat.

2. Meanwhile, in a medium bowl, combine 1/2 teaspoon salt, nutmeg, parsley, garlic, parmesan, 1 egg, and all of the pork. Form the meat mixture into balls, about a teaspoonful of meat per ball, as larger balls tend to break apart while cooking.

3. Once the stock is boiling, use a slotted spoon to carefully lower the balls into the pot. Place the lid on the pot and allow the soup to simmer until the meat is properly cooked, about 10 minutes.

4. In a separate bowl, whisk together the remaining salt and eggs with the bread crumbs and cream cheese. Pour the eggs through a colander into the hot soup. Whisk the eggs with chopsticks to disperse them while cooking.

5. Ladle the soup into bowls and serve.

SIMPLE MUSHROOM SOUP

COOK TIME: 30-40 MINS | MAKES: 4-6 SERVINGS

INGREDIENTS:

- 6 tbsp. butter
- 6 tbsp. vegetable oil
- 1 shallot, diced
- 2 tsp. crushed garlic
- 4 cups vegetable broth
- 1 1/2 lb. button mushrooms, cleaned and sliced
- kosher salt
- freshly ground black pepper
- 4 cups water
- 2 tbsp. tahini sauce

- 2 tbsp. soy sauce
- 1 tbsp. toasted sesame oil

DIRECTIONS:

1. Heat 1 tablespoon of butter and 1 tablespoon oil in a large cast-iron pot over medium heat. When the oil and butter combination is bubbling, add the shallots and cook until translucent, about 5 minutes. Stir in the garlic and allow the flavors to meld for about 1 minute. When the onions are just beginning to caramelize, whisk in the vegetable broth.

2. In a separate cast-iron pan, heat 1 tablespoon of oil and 1 tablespoon of butter over medium heat. When the butter and oil combination is hot, stir in the mushrooms and cook until they darken. Season to taste with salt and pepper before scrapping the contents of the pan into your pot of soup. You can do this in batches if your mushrooms do not comfortably fit in the pan, adding 1 tablespoon of butter and 1 table-spoon of oil each time.

3. Heat the water in your pan and loosen any bits of mushroom that may have stuck to the bottom before pouring the water into your soup. Stir in the tahini sauce and bring the soup to a simmer. Lower the heat and allow the soup to simmer for 15 minutes with the lid off the pot.

4. After 15 minutes, stir in the soy sauce and sesame oil. You can add more salt and pepper before serving if needed.

HEARTY BEEF STEW

COOK TIME: 2-3 HOURS | MAKES: 8-10 SERVINGS

INGREDIENTS:

- 1/2 cup all-purpose flour
- kosher salt
- freshly ground black pepper
- 5 lb. beef chuck, cut into 1 1/2" cubes
- 5 tbsp. Olive oil
- 3 shallots, diced
- 4 bay leaves
- 1/3 tsp. ground nutmeg
- 1 tsp. crushed thyme

- 1 tsp. dark brown sugar
- 2 cups beef broth
- 12 oz. O'Hara's Irish stout
- 1 lb. button mushrooms, cleaned and halved
- chopped parsley for garnish

DIRECTIONS:

1. In a large bowl, toss together the flour, 1/2 teaspoon salt, and 1/2 teaspoon pepper. Add the meat and continue to toss until all of the meat is covered in the flour.

2. Use a large cast-iron pot to heat the oil over high heat. Add the coated meat to the hot oil and cook for 10 minutes or until the meat is properly browned. Use a slotted spoon to transfer the cubes to a plate.

3. Caramelize the diced shallots in the oil and fat from the meat, about 4 minutes. Add the browned beef back to the pot and stir in the bay leaves, nutmeg, thyme, sugar, beef broth, stout, and mushrooms. Season with 2 teaspoons of salt and 1 teaspoon of pepper.

4. Once the stew is boiling, place the lid on the pot and lower the heat. Allow the tew to simmer for about 2 hours or until the meat is tender. Stirring occasionally to prevent burning. Remove the bay leaves and allow the stew to rest before ladling into bowls and garnishing with parsley before serving.

WINE BRAISED CHICKEN

COOK TIME: 1 1/2-2 HOURS | MAKES: 4-6 SERVINGS

INGREDIENTS:

- 1 tbsp. olive oil
- 6 oz. thick-cut bacon, cut into 1/2" cubes
- 3 1/2 lb. chicken, cut into 10 portions
- Himalayan salt
- white pepper
- 1 shallot, diced
- 2 spring onions, diced
- 12 oz. button mushrooms, cleaned and halved
- 2 tsp. crushed garlic

- 1 cup red wine
- 1 bay leaf
- 5 thyme sprigs
- 1 lb. carrots, sliced into 1/2" thick long strips
- 2 cups chicken broth
- 1 tbsp. rice wine vinegar
- 1 tbsp. butter
- chopped parsley for garnish

DIRECTIONS:

1. Set the oven to preheat at 350°F.

2. Heat the oil in a large cast-iron pot over medium heat before adding the bacon cubes. Brown the bacon for about 5 minutes or until the bacon is nice and crispy. Use a slotted spoon to transfer the bacon to a bowl lined with paper towels.

3. Place your chicken portions in a large bowl and season with a generous pinch of salt and pepper. Brown your chicken in the pot, skin side down, for 3-4 minutes or until the skin is a crispy brown. Do more than one batch as you don't want to overcrowd the pot. Transfer the browned chicken to a separate plate lined with paper towels.

4. Drain the majority of the oil from the pot, leaving about 2 tablespoons. Stir in the shallots, spring onions, and mushrooms. Cook for 4-6 minutes or until the mushrooms and shallots are tender. Stir in the garlic for 30 seconds. Pour the wine into the pot and use a wooden spoon to loosen any bits that may have stuck to the bottom. Stir in the bay leaf, thyme sprigs, carrot strips, and chicken broth. Season to taste with salt and pepper before stirring in the bacon and placing the chicken pieces carefully in the simmering pot. Cover the pot with tin foil and bake in the oven until the chicken is properly cooked about 1 1/2 hours.

5. Remove the pot from the oven and use a slotted spoon to transfer the chicken portions to a bowl. Return the pot to the plate over medium heat and stir until about half of the sauce has evaporated, approximately 5 minutes. Whisk in the butter and rice vinegar before adding the chicken once again.

6. Allow the chicken to rest in the pot for 5 minutes before ladling into bowls and topping with the chopped parsley.

TURKEY CHILI CON CARNE

COOK TIME: 3-5 HOURS | MAKES: 6-8 SERVINGS

INGREDIENTS:

- 1 lb. white soup beans
- 6 dried New Mexico chilies
- 1 tbsp. vegetable oil
- 1 shallot, chopped
- 2 tsp. ground cumin
- 2 tsp. crushed garlic
- 4-6 cups vegetable broth

- 1 smoked turkey leg
- kosher salt
- white pepper

DIRECTIONS:

1. Begin prepping your beans by fanning them out on a baking sheet and picking out anything that doesn't belong. Transfer the beans to a large cast-iron pot and cover with water. Bring the water to a boil and cook for 10 minutes before removing the pot from the heat and soaking the beans for 8 hours. Strain the soaked beans through a colander, rinse with fresh water and leave them to drain while you prepare the rest of the dish.

2. Cut the chilies into strips and remove the seeds. Submerge the chili strips in a bowl of hot water for 30 minutes. Transfer the chili strips along with 1 cup of the water they were soaking in, to a food processor. Pulse until you have a paste.

3. Set the oven to preheat at 325°F.

4. Heat the oil in a large cast-iron pot over medium heat and brown the shallots for 7-10 minutes or until they just begin to caramelize. Stir in the cumin and garlic for 1 minute, allowing the flavors to meld before adding the chili paste from the food processor.

5. Remove the turkey from the bone and dice the meat into small pieces. Stir the meat along with the soaked beans and 4 cups of vegetable broth into the pot. Bring the chili to a boil with the lid on the pot.

6. Transfer the pot to the oven and bake covered for 3-4 hours, stirring at 45-minute intervals. Keep an eye on the consistency of your chili, if there is too much liquid after 2 hours, uncover and continue to cook for the remainder of the time. If the moisture is evaporating too quickly, stir in more of the stock as needed.

7. Season to taste with salt and pepper.

SWEET & TANGY CHICKEN CURRY

COOK TIME: 30-40 MINS | MAKES: 4 SERVINGS

INGREDIENTS:

- 3 spring onions, finely chopped
- 3/4 tsp. white pepper
- 3/4 tsp. kosher salt
- 1/2 tsp. fish sauce
- 1 tsp. maple syrup
- 1 tsp. Worcestershire sauce
- 2 tsp. full-cream milk
- 2 tsp. soy sauce
- 4 tsp. toasted sesame oil
- 3 oz. white turnip, shredded

- 1 lb. chicken, minced
- 5 tsp. crushed garlic
- 1/4 cup grapeseed oil
- 1 large yellow onion, diced
- 2 stalks lemongrass, finely chopped
- 2 tsp. crushed ginger
- 1/2 tsp. ground turmeric
- 1/2 tsp. ground nutmeg
- 1/2 tsp. smoked paprika
- 1 tsp. ground cilantro seeds

- 1 tsp. ground cumin
- 1 tbsp. fish sauce
- 2 tbsp. soy sauce
- 2 tsp. cayenne pepper
- 1 cup coconut milk

DIRECTIONS:

1. In a large bowl, mix together the spring onions, pepper, salt, fish sauce, maple syrup, Worcestershire sauce, milk, soy sauce, sesame oil, turnip, chicken, and 1 teaspoon garlic. When everything is properly combined, form the mixture into balls, about 1 teaspoonful per ball.

2. Heat 1 tablespoon grapeseed oil in a large cast-iron skillet over medium heat. Divide the balls into batches and fry each batch for 4-5 minutes or until all the balls are browned in an even coat. Add 1 tablespoon of grapeseed oil with each additional batch. Place the cooked balls on a plate lined with paper towels and set aside.

3. Use greaseproof paper to clean your skillet, taking care not to burn. Return the skillet to the heat and warm 2 tablespoons of grapeseed oil. Stir in the onion, lemongrass, ginger, and 4 teaspoons of garlic and cook for a few minutes until the onions are tender.

4. Stir in the turmeric, nutmeg, paprika, cilantro seeds, cumin, fish sauce, soy sauce, and cayenne pepper. Allow the flavors to meld for 3 minutes, stirring continuously. Finally, mix in the coconut milk and use a handheld blender to blend any chunks in the sauce.

5. Bring the sauce to a simmer before adding the chicken balls and allowing them to cook for 3-4 minutes. Use a wooden spoon to stir the sauce until it thickens. Remove the skillet from the heat and season to taste with salt and pepper before serving.

SPICY BRUDET

COOK TIME: 1 HOUR | MAKES: 6-8 SERVINGS

INGREDIENTS:

- 1/4 cup olive oil
- 1 shallot, chopped
- 1/2 tsp. kosher salt
- 1 tsp. cayenne pepper
- 1 tsp. crushed basil
- 1 tsp. crushed oregano
- 4 tsp. crushed garlic
- 1 cup seafood broth
- 1 cup chicken broth
- 1 cup dry white wine
- 1/4 cup tomato purée
- 28 oz. peeled and drained tomatoes

- 1 lb. shrimp, shelled and deveined
- 1 lb. scallops, tough muscles removed
- 2 lb. king crab legs
- 1 lb. skinless cod fillets
- 1 lb. mussels, scrubbed
- 1 lb. clams, de-bearded
- flaky sea salt
- black pepper
- 1 loaf sourdough bread, sliced and toasted for serving

DIRECTIONS:

1. In a large cast-iron pot over medium heat, warm the oil before adding the chopped shallots and salt. Stir for about 10 minutes or until the shallots begin to caramelize. Stir in the cayenne pepper, basil, oregano, and garlic and allow the flavors to meld for 1 minute before adding the seafood broth, chicken broth, white wine, and tomato purée. Press the tomato through a sieve into the pan and remove any skins that may have been left behind. When the sauce begins to boil, reduce the heat and simmer for 30 minutes, stirring throughout.

2. Stir in the shrimp, scallops, crab legs, and fish fillets, cooking for 1o minutes. After 10 minutes add the mussels and clams, stirring for an additional 5-8 minutes. Remove and throw away any mussels and clams that have not opened while cooking.

3. Season to taste with salt and pepper. Serve in bowls with the bread on the side.

CORIANDER SHRIMP IN COCONUT MILK

COOK TIME: 15 MINS | MAKES: 6-8 SERVINGS

INGREDIENTS:

- Himalayan salt
- 3 lb. jumbo shrimp, shelled and deveined
- 2 tbsp. olive oil
- 1 red bell pepper, diced
- 1/2 tsp. cayenne pepper
- 4 tsp. crushed garlic
- 1/2 cup coriander leaves, chopped
- 4 spring onions, diced and colors separated

- 14 oz. coconut milk
- 14 oz. petite diced tomatoes, drained
- 2 tbsp. lime juice

DIRECTIONS:

1. Place the shrimp in a large bowl and season with 1 teaspoon of salt.

2. In a large cast-iron pot over medium heat, warm the olive oil before adding the bell peppers and frying for 4 minutes or until the peppers soften. Toss in the cayenne pepper, garlic, 1/4 cup of the coriander leaves, and the white parts of the spring onions, frying for 1 minute.

3. Stir in the coconut milk and tomatoes, bringing the sauce to a simmer. Lower the heat and stir for about 5 minutes or until the sauce thickens.

4. Stir in the shrimp and cook for an additional 5 minutes or until the shrimp blush and form a C. Remove the pot from the heat, stir in the lime juice, and season to taste with salt and pepper.

5. Serve the shrimp with the remaining coriander leaves and the green parts of the spring onions as garnish.

VEGETARIAN

CHEESY MUSHROOM & CHARD CASSEROLE

COOK TIME: 25-30 MINS | MAKES: 4 SERVINGS

INGREDIENTS:

- 4 oz. baguette, cut into 1/2" cubes
- 1 tbsp. butter
- 1 shallot, diced
- Himalayan salt
- white pepper
- 1 tsp. crushed thyme
- 1 tsp. crushed garlic
- 1 1/2 cups button mushrooms, cleaned and halved

- 4 cups chard, cleaned and diced
- 1 cup full-cream milk
- 4 large eggs
- 3/4 cups smoked mozzarella, shredded

DIRECTIONS:

1. Set the oven to preheat at 450°F with the wire rack in the center of the oven.

2. Fan the bread cubes out on a baking tray and bake for 3-5 minutes in the oven or until the cubes are a crispy brown.

3. In a large cast-iron pan over medium heat, melt the butter until it begins to bubble, and add the shallots. Fry until the shallots soften. Stir in 1/2 teaspoon salt, 1/2 teaspoon pepper, thyme, garlic, and mushrooms. Fry for about 3 minutes or until the mushrooms darken, stirring throughout. Add the chard to the pan and cook until it reduces in size, approximately 2 additional minutes.

4. Whisk together the milk, eggs, 1/2 teaspoon salt, and 1/4 teaspoon pepper in a medium bowl. Add the cheese and crisped bread, stirring until everything is properly combined before pouring the mixture into the pan.

5. Use the back of a wooden spoon to lightly press the mixture into the pan. Cover the pan with tin foil and bake in the oven for 10 minutes. Remove the foil after 10 minutes and continue to bake for an additional 5 minutes or until the top is golden brown.

6. Allow the casserole to rest for a few minutes before serving.

FRENCH-STYLE HOT DISH

COOK TIME: 1 1/2-2 HOURS | MAKES: 6-8 SERVINGS

INGREDIENTS:

- 5 tbsp. olive oil
- 2 bay leaves
- 1/2 tsp. crushed oregano
- 1/2 tsp. crushed thyme
- 1 tsp. crushed rosemary
- 2 shallots, chopped
- 4 tsp. crushed garlic
- 3 cups sweet red wine (more if needed)
- 2 cups canned tomatoes, diced
- 2 potatoes, peeled and diced

- 2 spring onions, chopped
- 2 carrots, diced
- kosher salt
- white pepper
- 1 large garlic clove, peeled
- butter
- 15 oz. canned white pea beans, drained and rinsed
- 1 cup tomato purée
- 1 cup panko breadcrumbs

DIRECTIONS:

1. Set the oven to preheat at 350°.

2. In a large cast-iron pot, heat the oil over medium-low heat. When the oil is hot, add the bay leaves, oregano, thyme, rosemary, shallots, and garlic. Stirring while allowing the fragrances to meld for 2 minutes.

3. Add the wine to the pot and raise the heat, bringing the sauce to a simmer. Place the lid on the pot and allow the ingredients to marinate for about 5 minutes or until the onions are tender.

4. When the onions are tender, stir in the tomatoes, potatoes, spring onions, carrots, and a large pinch of salt and pepper. Replace the lid and simmer for an additional 1o minutes or until the vegetables are soft. Remove the bay leaves and discard.

5. Chop the end off of the garlic clove and use it to season the inside of a large cast-iron casserole dish. Discard the garlic clove and generously butter the inside of the dish.

6. Ladle some of the vegetables and sauce into the bottom of the casserole dish and top with a layer of the beans. Repeat the process with 2 or 3 layers until all of the vegetables and beans have been used. Add the tomato purée as the top layer, ending with a layer of bread crumbs.

7. Cover the casserole dish in foil and bake in the oven for 1 1/2 hours, checking every 20 minutes to ensure that the casserole isn't drying out. Add more if it seems too dry.

8. Serve straight away.

CHEESY PAN TEMPEH

COOK TIME: 15 MINS | MAKES: 4 SERVINGS

INGREDIENTS:

- 1/2 tsp. kosher salt
- 1 tsp. red pepper flakes
- 1 tsp. ground cumin
- 1/2 tsp. cayenne pepper
- 1/2 tsp. chipotle powder
- 3 tsp. crushed garlic
- 1 tbsp. tomato purée
- 8 oz. tempeh, crumbled
- 2 tbsp. olive oil
- 1 shallot, diced

- 1 cup white rice, cooked
- 15 oz. black turtle beans drained and rinsed
- 1 cup mozzarella, grated
- 1 avocado, peeled, pitted, and sliced
- 12 baby tomatoes, halved
- 1 cup coriander leaves, chopped
- 1 lime, juiced
- Himalayan salt
- freshly ground black pepper
- hot sauce

DIRECTIONS:

1. Use a large bowl to combine the salt, red pepper flakes, cumin, cayenne pepper, chipotle powder, garlic, tomato purée, and tempeh.

2. Heat a cast-iron pan over medium heat before adding the olive oil and shallots. Fry for 3-4 minutes or until the shallots begin to caramelize. Stir in the spiced tempeh.

3. Toss the tempeh in the pan for about 5 minutes or until the edges are nicely crisped. Add the rice and beans, mixing for 2-3 minutes until everything is properly combined.

4. Add the mozzarella and wait for the cheese to melt. Remove the pan from the stove.

5. Layer the avocado slices, baby tomatoes, and coriander leaves on top of the melted cheese. Drizzle with lime juice and a pinch of salt and pepper.

6. Serve in the middle of the table with an optional side of hot sauce.

SPRINGTIME ARBORIO RISOTTO

COOK TIME: 15-20 MINS | MAKES: 4-6 SERVINGS

INGREDIENTS:

- 7 cups vegetable stock
- Himalayan salt
- freshly ground black pepper
- 1/4 cup extra-virgin olive oil
- 2 tsp. crushed garlic
- 1 1/4 cup yellow onions, diced
- 7 oz. button mushrooms, cleaned and sliced

- 1 3/4 cups arborio rice
- 1/2 cup dry white wine
- 1 cup asparagus stalks, trimmed and cut
- 1 cup parmesan, shredded

DIRECTIONS:

1. In a medium cast-iron pot over high heat, bring the vegetable stock to a simmer and season to taste with salt and pepper. Keep an eye on the heat while you prepare the rest of the dish.

2. While the stock is simmering, heat the oil in a large cast-iron pot over medium-high heat. Stir in the garlic and onions and fry for about 3 minutes or until the onions are fork-tender. Stir in the mushrooms and fry for about 2 minutes or until the mushrooms have darkened.

3. Toss in the rice and roast for about 3 minutes, tossing throughout, or until the rice is lightly browned.

4. Pour in the wine and stir the rice for about 30 seconds, most of the wine should have been absorbed during that time.

5. Transfer about 1 1/2 cups of the vegetable broth to your rice pot. Stir the rice for about 1 minute or until most of the stock has been absorbed. Stir in another 1 1/2 cups of stock and repeat the process until the rice is al dente. It should take about 3 batches of stock.

6. Add the asparagus and 1 cup of stock to the pot and cook for about 5 minutes or until the asparagus is tender but not completely soft.

7. Transfer the pot to a wooden chopping board and stir in the parmesan. All the Risotto to rest for about 5 minutes before serving.

BAKED YAM TORTILLAS

COOK TIME: 1 HOUR | MAKES: 6-8 SERVINGS

INGREDIENTS:

- 1 green bird's eye chili, seeded and chopped
- 4 tsp. garlic cloves, quartered
- 2 shallots, quartered
- 2 lb. tomatillos, husks removed
- 1/4 cup olive oil
- Himalayan salt
- white pepper
- 2 tsp. cayenne pepper
- 1 tsp. ground cumin
- 1 lb. yams, peeled and chopped
- 1/2 cup coriander leaves, chopped (Extra for garnish)
- 1 cup vegetable broth
- 1 tbsp. lime juice
- 8 oz. mozzarella, shredded
- 8 oz. edam, shredded
- 15 oz. turtle beans, drained and rinsed
- 10 corn tortillas
- sour cream

DIRECTIONS:

1. Set the oven to preheat at 400°F.
2. In a large bowl, toss together the chili, garlic, shallots, tomatillos, 2 tablespoons olive oil, and season with salt and pepper. Fan the ingredients out on a baking tray and set aside.
3. Using the same bowl, toss together the cayenne pepper, cumin, yams, remaining olive oil, and season with salt and pepper. Fan the yams out on a separate baking pan. Place both pans in the oven and bake for 15 minutes before turning all of the vegetables and baking for an additional 15 minutes or until the vegetables are fork-tender. Set aside half of the shallots and half of the garlic.
4. Pulse the contents of the tomatillo pan in a food processor and add the coriander leaves, broth, and a pinch of salt and pepper. Pour the sauce into a cast-iron skillet and bring to a simmer for 4-6 minutes. Remove the skillet from the heat and whisk in the lime juice. Season to taste if needed.
5. Toss the two kinds of cheese together in a bowl and set aside.
6. Chop the garlic and shallots that were set aside and toss them together in a large bowl with the yams, beans, and 1 1/2 cup of the mixed cheese.
7. Coat the inside of each tortilla with about 1 tablespoon of the tomatillo sauce. Place about 1/2 cup of the bean mixture in the middle of the tortilla and fold into a burrito with the ends closed. Place your wrapped tortillas in a cast-iron baking dish and top with about 1/2 cup of the sauce. Reserve the rest as a dip for serving. Sprinkle the remaining cheese over the tortillas. Cover the bowl in tin foil and bake in the oven for 30 minutes. Remove the foil and return the dish to the oven for an additional 5 minutes or until the cheese is melted and lightly toasted.
8. Dollop the sour cream over the tortillas and garnish with the rest of the coriander before serving with the sauce on the side.

VEGETARIAN RAGOUT

COOK TIME: 20-30 MINS | MAKES: 4 SERVINGS

INGREDIENTS:

- 1 1/2 cups warm water
- 1/2 cup dried porcini mushrooms
- 2 tbsp. olive oil
- 3 tbsp. butter
- 1 cup yellow onions, diced
- flaky sea salt
- 2 lb. button mushrooms, cleaned and diced
- 1/2 cup dry vermouth
- 2 tbsp. heavy cream

- 1/4 cup herbs, parsley, oregano, thyme, chives, sage
- white pepper
- 3 1/2 cups cold water
- 1 cup instant polenta
- 1/4 cup cream cheese
- 1/2 cup parmesan, shredded

DIRECTIONS:

1. Place the dried mushrooms in a small bowl and cover with the warm water. Once the mushrooms have rehydrated, about 10 minutes, use a slotted spoon to transfer them to a wooden board. Set aside 1 cup of the water and chop the mushrooms.

2. Heat the olive oil and 1 tablespoon butter in a large cast-iron pot over medium heat. When the butter and oil is bubbling, stir in the shallots for about 4 minutes or until they begin to caramelize. Stir in the button mushrooms and fry for about 6 minutes or until the mushrooms begin to darken. Stir in the porcini mushrooms for 3-4 minutes or until they are fork-tender.

3. Pour in the vermouth and stir until all of the juice has cooked away, about 2 minutes. Strain 1 cup of the reserved water, removing any debris, pour the water into the pot, and cook for 3-4 minutes or until the liquid has reduced by 3/4 cups.

4. Whisk in the cream and mixed herbs. Add a pinch of salt and pepper if needed. Remove the pot from the heat and set aside with the lid on.

5. In a separate cast-iron pot over medium heat, bring the cold water to a boil with 1 1/2 tsp. Salt. When the water is boiling, stir in the polenta. Reduce the heat and allow the polenta to simmer for about 3 minutes or until all of the water has been absorbed. Whisk in 2 tbsp. butter and cream cheese. Stir in the parmesan.

6. Serve the mushroom ragout on a bed of polenta.

MUSHROOM & CHARD CURRY

COOK TIME: 35 MINS | MAKES: 4 SERVINGS

INGREDIENTS:

- 2 cups vegetable stock
- 1/4 cup Thai green curry paste
- 1 large yam, peeled and cubed
- 8 oz. chard, cleaned and chopped
- 8 oz. button mushrooms, cleaned and chopped
- 4 lb. haricot verts, stems removed
- 1 can coconut milk
- 1 lime, juiced
- cooked rice for serving

DIRECTIONS:

1. Heat a cast-iron pan over medium heat before pouring in the stock and curry paste, whisking until everything is properly combined.

2. Add the yams and cook for 15-20 minutes or until they are fork-tender. Stir every few minutes to prevent burning.

3. Stir in the chard, mushrooms, and haricot verts. Cook for 5-7 minutes while stirring.

4. Lower the heat until the pan is gently simmering. Stir in the coconut milk and lime juice, allow the curry to simmer for 2-3 minutes while stirring.

5. Serve the curry over a bed of cooked rice.

POACHED EGGS ON TORTILLAS

COOK TIME: 10 MINS | MAKES: 4 SERVINGS

INGREDIENTS:

- 2 limes, juiced
- kosher salt
- freshly ground black pepper
- 1/2 cup coriander leaves, chopped
- 2 tsp. crushed garlic
- 1/2 purple onion, chopped
- 1 jalapeño chili, chopped
- 2 cups cherry tomatoes, quartered
- 2 cups turtle beans

- 1 teaspoon cayenne pepper
- 1 tbsp. olive oil
- 4 corn tortillas
- 8 oz. mozzarella, divided into 4 helpings (plus a little extra for garnish)
- 4 large eggs
- 1 avocado, peeled, pitted, and sliced

DIRECTIONS:

1. In a large bowl, toss together the lime juice, 1/2 teaspoon salt, 1/2 teaspoon pepper, coriander leaves, garlic, onion, chili, and tomatoes. Set aside.

2. In a medium cast-iron pot over medium heat, stir together the beans, cayenne pepper, and a generous amount of salt and pepper. Stir until the beans are cooked.

3. Heat a cast-iron pan over medium heat before adding the oil.

4. Add one tortilla to the center of the pan and top with 1 helping of cheese. Make a well in the center of the cheese and crack the egg into the well, taking care not to damage the yolk. Season the egg with a pinch of salt and pepper. Cook until the white is no longer runny.

5. Gently shift a spatula under the tortilla, making sure to support the egg, flip the tortilla in one fluid movement.

6. Cook the other side for 2-3 minutes, if you prefer a firmer yolk, cook the egg for 4-5 minutes. Transfer the poached tortilla egg to a plate.

7. Repeat the process with the remaining tortillas and eggs.

8. Garnish the eggs with beans, salsa, avocado, and cheese before serving.

TEMPEH STIR-FRY

COOK TIME: 10 MINS | MAKES: 2 SERVINGS

INGREDIENTS:

- 2 tsp. soy sauce
- 2 tbsp. black bean paste
- 4 tsp. crushed garlic
- 1/2 cup and 1 1/2 tsp. cold water
- 2 tbsp. peanut oil
- 1 lb. tempeh, drained and cubed (1" cubes)
- 3 oz. oyster mushrooms, cleaned and diced
- 4 bunches baby Bok choy, stems removed and sliced into 1/2" strips
- 1 1/2 tsp. corn flour
- cooked basmati rice for serving
- 1 spring onion, chopped

DIRECTIONS:

1. In a small bowl, whisk together the soy sauce, black bean paste, 2 teaspoons garlic, and 1/2 cup water. Set aside on the counter while you prepare the rest of the dish.

2. Pour the oil into a cast-iron wok, when the oil is hot, fry the tempeh for 5 minutes or until nicely browned, tossing throughout. Toss in the remaining garlic and let the flavors meld for 1 minute.

3. Toss in and fry the mushrooms and Bok choy for 1 minute. Pour in the black bean paste sauce and toss to coat the tempeh for 1 minute.

4. In a small glass bowl, whisk together the corn flour and remaining water until all the lumps are gone. Stir the mixture into the wok and toss for 1 minute or until the sauce begins to thicken.

5. Serve the tempeh on a bed of rice and garnish with the spring onions.

LAYERED VEGETABLES WITH PESTO

COOK TIME: 45-60 MINS | MAKES: 4 SERVINGS

INGREDIENTS:

- 2 bay leaves
- 3 tbsp. bay leaves
- 6 sage leaves
- 3 thyme sprigs
- 7 plump garlic cloves, halved
- 2 shallots, chopped into large chunks
- 3/4 lb. carrots, cut into 2" strips
- 3/4 lb. baby potatoes, peeled and quartered
- 1/2 lb. haricot verts, trimmed
- 1 yellow bell pepper, seeded and cut into 1" strips
- 1 lb. butternut, cut into 1" rounds
- 5 heirloom tomatoes, skins removed and cut into crescents
- 15 oz. canned navy beans, rinsed and drained
- kosher salt
- freshly ground black pepper
- 1/2 cup parmesan, shredded
- 3 tbsp. water
- 6 tbsp. olive oil
- 2 garlic cloves
- 1 cup packed basil leaves

DIRECTIONS:

1. Heat the bay leaves and olive oil in a large cast-iron pot over medium heat. When the fragrance is released from the leaves, stir in the sage, thyme, garlic, and shallots.

2. Beginning with the potatoes, place each vegetable in a single layer, seasoning each layer with salt and pepper as you work. End the layers with the peeled tomatoes and any juice that may have accumulated in the bowl. Cover the pot and cook the vegetables for 45-60 minutes or until the vegetables are fork-tender. To check the vegetables gently slide a knife through the layers, this recipe does not require any stirring. If it seems like the pot is too dry you can add a few tablespoons of water, but this should not happen if the vegetables were packed in their own layers.

3. Place the parmesan, water, oil, garlic, and basil leaves in a food processor. Pulse to form a paste, season with salt and pepper to taste.

4. Serve the vegetables hot with the pesto as garnish.

CHEESY MUSHROOM LASAGNA

COOK TIME: 1 HOUR | MAKES: 6-8 SERVINGS

INGREDIENTS:

- 2 tbsp. olive oil
- 2 lb. oyster mushrooms, cleaned and diced
- 1 large yellow onion, chopped
- 1/4 cup butter
- 1/4 cup all-purpose flour
- 3 cups full-cream milk
- 1/3 tsp. ground nutmeg
- 1 tbsp. Crushed thyme
- 2 large eggs
- 2 cups cream cheese

- 2 1/2 cups mozzarella, shredded
- 2 cups cheddar, shredded
- 12 oz. instant lasagna sheets
- 1/2 cup parmesan, shredded

DIRECTIONS:

1. Set the oven to preheat at 400°F.

2. Heat a large cast-iron skillet over medium heat before adding the oil and frying the mushrooms in portions for 2-4 minutes per portion or until the mushrooms darken. Transfer the cooked mushrooms to a bowl and sprinkle with a pinch of salt. Set aside.

3. Fry the onions in the same skillet for half a minute. Add the butter to the skillet. When the butter is bubbling, whisk in the flour to form a paste and cook for a few minutes until the paste has browned. Gradually whisk in the milk and cook for 2-3 minutes. When the sauce thickens, whisk in the nutmeg and season to taste with salt and pepper. Scrape the white sauce into a clean bowl and set aside.

4. In a small bowl, whisk together the thyme, eggs, and cream cheese. Use a second bowl to mix the mozzarella and cheddar.

5. In a large cast-iron casserole dish, begin layering the lasagna by starting with a layer of the white sauce, then noodles, a layer of the cream cheese, cooked mushroom, and the mixed cheeses. Repeat the layers until all of the ingredients have been used, ending with a layer of the mozzarella and cheddar.

6. Cover the dish and bake for 30-40 minutes before removing the foil and baking for an additional 10 minutes. The cheese on top should be nice and bubbly.

7. Allow the lasagna to cool for 10 minutes on the counter before sprinkling with the parmesan and serving.

DESSERTS

BUTTERY PEACH CAKE

COOK TIME: 45 MINS | MAKES: 8 SERVINGS

INGREDIENTS:

- 1/2 cup butter, melted
- 1 1/2 tsp. ground cinnamon
- 1/2 tsp. nutmeg
- 1/2 cup fine white sugar
- 1/2 cup dark brown sugar
- 1 1/2 cups all-purpose flour
- 1/2 tsp. baking powder
- 1/2 tsp. bicarbonate of soda
- 1 1/4 cups all-purpose flour

- 1/2 white sugar
- 1/2 cup butter, room temperature
- 1 1/2 tsp. vanilla essence
- 2 large eggs
- 1/2 cup sour cream
- 1 lb. canned peaches, drained and sliced

DIRECTIONS:

1. Use butter to generously grease a 10-inch cast-iron pan and set the oven to preheat at 350°F.

2. In a large bowl, combine 1/2 cup butter, cinnamon, nutmeg, 1/2 cup white sugar, 1/2 cup brown sugar, and 1 1/2 cups flour. Use clean hands to crumble the mixture between your fingers and create fine bread crumbs that resemble wet sand. Set aside while you prepare the rest of the cake.

3. In a small ball, whisk together the baking powder, bicarbonate of soda, and 1 1/4 cup flour. In a separate bowl, beat the sugar and butter until the mixture is light and fluffy. Beat in the vanilla, eggs, and sour cream. Gradually add the flour mixture to the batter and beat until you have a lump-free mixture.

4. Use an offset spatula to scrape the batter into the greased pan and smooth it out. Decorate the top of the batter with the peach slices. Break apart any clumps that may have formed in your crumble mixture and sprinkle the crumbs over the peaches in an even layer.

5. Place the pan in the oven and bake for 45 minutes or until an inserted skewer comes out clean and the crumb topping is golden brown. The peaches keep the cake moist so there may still be a bit of crumbs stuck to the skewer when removed from the cake. This is alright.

6. Allow the cake to sit in the pan for a few minutes before serving.

VERY-BERRY PIE

COOK TIME: 55-60 MINS | MAKES: 6 SERVINGS

INGREDIENTS:

- 3 tbsp. corn flour
- 3/4 cups white sugar
- 1 cup blueberries
- 1 cup raspberries
- 3 cups strawberries, hulled and sliced
- 1/4 tsp. kosher salt
- 1/4 tsp. bicarbonate of soda
- 1/2 tsp. baking powder

- 1 1/4 cups all-purpose flour
- 2/3 cups dark brown sugar
- 1/4 cup unsalted butter
- 1/2 tsp. vanilla essence
- 1 large egg
- 3/4 cups buttermilk
- whipped cream for serving

DIRECTIONS:

1. Set the oven to preheat at 350°F.

2. Whisk together the corn flour and white sugar in a large bowl, stir in the blueberries, raspberries, and strawberries. Transfer the mixture to a large cast-iron pan and set aside.

3. In a clean bowl, whisk together the salt, bicarbonate of soda, baking powder, and all-purpose flour.

4. In a clean bowl, beat the brown sugar and butter until the mixture is light and fluffy. Beat in the vanilla and egg. Beat in half off the flour until properly combined before beating in the buttermilk. Add the remaining flour and beat until you have a lump-free batter.

5. Gently dollop the batter over the berries in the pan until all of the berries are covered with the batter, do not stir.

6. Place the pan in the oven and bake for 55-60 minutes or until an inserted skewer comes out clean and the top is nicely browned.

7. Serve hot with a large dollop of whipped cream.

DECADENT TIPSY BREAD PUDDING

COOK TIME: 45 MINS | MAKES: 4-6 SERVINGS

INGREDIENTS:

- 1 French loaf, cut into 1-inch cubes
- 1 cup semisweet chocolate chips
- 1/4 tsp. vanilla essence
- 1/4 tsp. ground ginger
- 1/4 tsp. ground nutmeg
- 1/4 tsp. ground cinnamon
- 1/2 cup fine white sugar
- 1 cup heavy cream
- 2 cups full-cream milk

- 5 large eggs
- 1/2 cup dark brown sugar
- 2 tbsp. butter
- 2 cups heavy cream
- 2 tbsp. corn flour
- 3/4 cups brandy
- 1 tsp. vanilla essence
- 1 tbsp. confectioners' sugar
- 1 cup heavy whipping cream

DIRECTIONS:

1. Set the oven to preheat at 350°F and generally grease the inside of a 12-inch cast-iron pan.

2. Place the bread cubes in a single layer in your buttered pan and sprinkle with the chocolate chips.

3. Beat the vanilla, ginger, nutmeg, cinnamon, white sugar, heavy cream, full-cream milk, and eggs in a large bowl. Gently pour the mixture into the pan, soaking the bread. Do not stir.

4. Place the pan in the oven and bake for 45 minutes or until the pudding is golden brown.

5. Meanwhile, heat the dark brown sugar, butter, and heavy cream in a cast-iron pot over medium heat, reduce the heat if the mixture begins to simmer, you do not want the sauce to boil.

6. In a small bowl, briskly whisk together the corn flour and brandy until properly combined. Drizzle the brandy into the pot while whisking, until the sauce thickens. Place the pot on a wooden chopping board to cool.

7. Beat the vanilla, confectioners' sugar, and whipping cream in a medium bowl, until soft peaks form. Place the whipped cream in the fridge until the pudding is ready to serve.

8. Once the pudding is ready, place the pan on a wire rack and pour the brandy sauce over the top. Allow the pudding to cool for about 20 minutes. Dollop with the whipped cream and serve.

PEACH & BLUEBERRY TARTE TIN

COOK TIME: 30-50 MINS | MAKES: 8-10 SERVINGS

INGREDIENTS:

- 1/2 tsp. ground nutmeg
- 1/2 tsp. ground ginger
- 1 cup dark brown sugar
- 1/3 tsp. kosher salt
- 1/3 cup butter
- 1 cup blueberries, stems removed
- 4 cans sliced peaches, drained
- 1/4 tsp. ground ginger
- 1/2 tsp. ground nutmeg

- 1/2 tsp. ground cinnamon
- 1/3 tsp. kosher salt
- 1/4 tsp. bicarbonate of soda
- 1 tsp. baking powder
- 1 1/2 cups all-purpose flour
- 1/2 cup white sugar
- 1/3 cup butter
- 1 tsp. vanilla essence
- 1/2 tsp. fresh ginger, grated

- 1/4 cup raw honey
- 1/3 cup full-cream milk
- 2 large eggs
- 1/2 tsp. ground ginger
- 1/2 tsp. vanilla essence
- 2 tbsp. confectioner's sugar
- 1 cup cold heavy cream
- candied peel for garnish

DIRECTIONS:

1. Set the oven to preheat at 350°F with the wire rack in the middle of the oven. Place a large, empty bowl in the fridge.

2. In a deep cast-iron pan over medium heat, whisk together 1/4 teaspoon nutmeg, 1/2 teaspoon ginger, 1 cup dark brown sugar, and 1/3 cup of butter, allow the mixture to cook for 3-4 minutes until the sauce darkens and all the sugar granules have melted, whisking continuously to prevent burning. Set the pan aside on a wooden chopping board.

3. Carefully arrange the blueberries and peaches in the skillet with the caramel sauce. This will be the top of the cake. In this recipe, we placed the peach halves on the outside of the pan and the blueberries in the center to form a flower.

4. In a large bowl, sift together 1/4 teaspoon ginger, 1/2 teaspoon nutmeg, 1/2 teaspoon cinnamon, 1/3 teaspoon salt, 1/4 teaspoon bicarbonate of soda, 1 teaspoon baking powder, and flour, set aside. Beat in the vanilla, fresh ginger, and honey.

5. In a large bowl, beat the white sugar and 1/3 cup butter until the mixture is light and fluffy. Gradually beat in the milk and eggs before beating in the flour mixture until you have a lump-free batter.

6. Very carefully dollop the batter into your pan on top of your fruit arrangement, taking care not to shift the fruit. Use an offset spatula to smooth out the top. Bake in the oven for 30-45 minutes or until an inserted skewer comes out clean and the top is golden brown.

7. Allow the cake to cool in the pan on a wire rack for 5 minutes before placing a plate over the pan and flipping in one fluid motion. Gently fix any fruit that may have shifted during the flipping process. The pan will still be hot so take care not to burn and use oven gloves.

8. Remove your cold bowl from the fridge and beat the ginger, vanilla, confectioner's sugar, and heavy cream until stiff peaks form. Garnish the cake with candied peel and serve with a side of the whipped cream.

MOIST ALMOND WHISKY CAKE

COOK TIME: 50-55 MINS | MAKES: 6-8 SERVINGS

INGREDIENTS:

- 5 ripe nectarines, pitted
- 1 tsp. crushed thyme
- 3/4 tsp. salt
- 1 tsp. baking powder
- 3/4 cups almond meal
- 1 cup all-purpose flour
- 3/4 cups white sugar
- 1 cup butter
- 2 large eggs

- 1 tbsp. Single malt whisky
- 1/2 cup plain, unsweetened yogurt
- 3 tbsp. dark brown sugar
- whipped cream for serving

DIRECTIONS:

1. Set the oven to preheat at 350°F. Generously grease a deep cast-iron pan with butter. Measure and cut a piece of greaseproof paper bigger than the pan to hang over the sides when pressed inside. Press the greaseproof paper into the pan.

2. Slice one nectarine into crescents and set aside. Chop the remaining nectarines into small cubes.

3. In a large bowl, whisk together the thyme, salt, baking powder, almond meal, and all-purpose flour.

4. Beat the sugar and butter to incorporate as much air as possible, about 5 minutes. Gradually beat in the eggs, beating for an additional 5 minutes before pushing the batter down and adding the flour mixture. When the flour is properly incorporated, whisk in the whisky and yogurt until the batter is smooth. Gently stir in the chopped nectarines using a wooden spoon.

5. Pour the batter into your prepared pan. Smoothing out the top. Use the sliced nectarines to decorate the top.

6. Sprinkle the sugar over the nectarine slices and place the pan in the oven for 50-55 minutes or until an inserted skewer comes out clean. Rotate the pan halfway through baking.

7. Allow the cake to cool completely in the pan before serving with a large dollop of whipped cream.

SWEET CINNAMON PEAR FRITTERS

COOK TIME: 60 MINS | MAKES: 40 FRITTERS

INGREDIENTS:

- 20 tsp. ground cinnamon
- 1 1/2 cups dark brown sugar (Plus 1 tbsp.)
- 1/2 tsp. lemon rind, finely grated
- 2 tsp. ground ginger
- 2 ripe pears, cored and finely chopped
- 3 large egg whites
- 1 tsp. vanilla essence

- 1 cup full-cream milk
- 1 1/2 cups all-purpose flour
- 2 cups sunflower oil

DIRECTIONS:

1. In a medium bowl, whisk together 18 teaspoons ground cinnamon, 1 tablespoon dark brown sugar, lemon rind, and ginger. Stir in the chopped pears and set aside.

2. In a separate bowl, beat the egg whites until soft peaks start to form.

3. In a third bowl, beat the vanilla, milk, and 1/2 cup of the dark brown sugar until you have incorporated as much air as possible and all of the sugar granules have dissolved. Beat in the flour until the mixture just comes together, do not over mix. Fold in the egg whites using an offset spatula before folding in the chopped pears.

4. In a small bowl, whisk together the rest of the cinnamon and sugar.

5. In a large cast-iron pot, heat the oil over medium heat until the tip of a wooden skewer immediately begins to sizzle when inserted.

6. Use an ice cream scoop to gently drop portions of the batter into the oil. Do not try to fry too many at once. 3 or 4 at a time is perfect. Deep fry the batter balls for 2 minutes before turning in the oil and frying the other sides for an additional 2 minutes or until the balls are golden brown in an even layer.

7. Place the balls in a bowl lined with paper towels. Once all of the balls are done, transfer the fritters to a clean bowl and toss in the cinnamon sugar. Serve immediately.

CHOCOLATE PEANUT-BUTTER PAN BROWNIES

COOK TIME: 35-40 MINS | MAKES: 8 SERVINGS

INGREDIENTS:

- 1/4 tsp. kosher salt
- 1/2 tsp. baking powder
- 2/3 cups rice flour
- 1/2 cup cocoa powder
- 1 cup dark brown sugar
- 1/2 cup dairy milk chocolate, roughly chopped
- 1 cup salted butter

- 2 tsp. vanilla essence
- 2 large eggs
- 1 tbsp. icing sugar
- 1/4 cup chunky peanut butter
- 1 tbsp. full-cream milk (more if needed)

DIRECTIONS:

1. Use butter grease the inside of an 8-inch cast-iron pan and set the oven to preheat at 350°F.

2. Sift together the salt, baking powder, rice flour, and cocoa powder in a medium bowl. Stir in the sugar.

3. Melt the chocolate and butter in a small cast-iron pot over medium heat. When the butter and chocolate is properly combined, transfer the pot to a wooden chopping board and briskly whisk in the vanilla and eggs. Stirn in the flour mixture until you have a lump-free batter.

4. Scrape the brownie batter into your greased pan and use an offset spatula to smooth out the surface.

5. In a small bowl, whisk together the icing sugar, peanut butter, and milk until you have a smooth frosting. You can add extra milk if the frosting seems too thick to pipe.

6. Transfer the peanut butter frosting to a piping bag and pipe it over the brownie mixture in your desired pattern.

7. Place the pan in the oven and bake for 35-40 minutes or until an inserted skewer comes out clean.

8. Allow the brownies to cool completely in the pan before slicing and serving.

BLUEBERRY POUND CAKE

COOK TIME: 1 HOUR 20 MINS | MAKES: 6-8 SERVINGS

INGREDIENTS:

- 2 1/2 cups dark brown sugar
- 1 lb. butter (extra for greasing)
- 1 tsp. vanilla essence
- 6 large eggs
- 1/4 tsp. ground nutmeg
- 1 teaspoon kosher salt
- 2 tsp. baking powder

- 3 1/2 cups all-purpose flour
- 1 cup buttermilk
- 1 lemon, juiced
- 1 tbsp. white sugar
- 2 cups blueberries

DIRECTIONS:

1. Set the oven to preheat at 325°F. Use butter to generously grease a 12-inch cast-iron pan.

2. In a bowl, beat the sugar and butter until the mixture is light and fluffy. Gradually beat in the vanilla and eggs until everything is properly combined.

3. In a separate bowl, whisk together the nutmeg, salt, baking powder, and flour.

4. Alternating between the flour and buttermilk, gradually beat in the ingredients until you have a lump-free batter.

5. Scrape the batter into your prepared pan, smoothing out the top using an offset spatula. Place the pan in the oven and bake for 1 hour and 15 minutes or until the top is golden brown and an inserted skewer comes out clean.

6. Meanwhile, in a small cast-iron pot over medium heat, whisk together the lemon juice, white sugar, and blueberries. Bring the mixture to a gentle simmer, stirring throughout until the liquid has reduced by half and you have a thick jam. Set aside off the heat.

7. When the cake is done, allow it to cool in the pan for 15 minutes before topping with the jam and serving.

UPSIDE-DOWN APPLE PIE

COOK TIME: 1 HOUR | MAKES: 8-10 SERVINGS

INGREDIENTS:

- 1/2 tsp. salt
- 3 tbsp. fine white sugar
- 1 1/2 cups all-purpose flour (extra for dusting)
- 5 tbsp. cold butter, cubed
- 3 tbsp. ice water
- 1/2 tsp. vanilla essence

- 1 large egg yolk
- 1/8 tsp. salt
- 3/4 cups dark brown sugar
- 7 tbsp. butter
- 6 red apples, peeled, cored, and halved
- whipped cream for serving

DIRECTIONS:

1. Sift together 1/2 teaspoon salt, 3 tablespoons white sugar, and 1 1/2 cups all-purpose flour. Transfer to a blender and pulse with 5 tablespoons butter until your mixture resembles coarse sand. In a small bowl, beat 3 tablespoons ice water, 1/2 teaspoon vanilla, and 1 egg yolk before pouring it into the blender. Blend until all the ingredients come together. Transfer your dough to a lightly floured surface and knead until your dough is smooth and elastic. Gather the dough into a smooth ball and seal with cling-wrap. Place the ball in the fridge for 15-30 minutes.

2. In a large cast-iron pan over medium heat, melt 1/8 teaspoon salt, 3/4 cups dark brown sugar, and 7 tablespoons butter. Stir with a wooden spoon until all of the sugar granules melt and the mixture darkens. Transfer the pan to a wooden chopping board.

3. Reserve 4 of the apple halves. Carefully arrange the remaining apple halves in the caramel sauce, flat sides down, place them as close together as possible.

4. Return the pan to the stove on medium heat and allow the apples to cook undisturbed until the bottoms are golden brown. Watch the heat, if the sugar begins to burn, turn it down. Carefully flip the apples and allow the other sides to brown. Gently turn the pan and shift the sugar as they cook.

5. Carefully remove the majority of the caramel sauce from the pan, pouring it into a separate pan. You should leave about 1-inch of the sauce with the apples. Place the reserved apple halves in the pan and brown them on both sides. Stirring and flipping when needed.

6. Carefully pour all of the caramel sauce into the pan of sauce from earlier, using a spatula to hold back the apples. Cook the apples on their own until they are all-fork tender and nicely browned. The entire apple browning process should take about 35 minutes from start to finish.

7. Transfer the pan to a wooden chopping board after pouring any excess liquid into the other pan. Allow the apples to cool completely. When the apples are cool, arrange them in the pan according to a design of your choice.

8. Set the oven to preheat at 375°F.

9. On a lightly floured surface, roll out the dough so that your dough is 1-inch bigger than the pan right around. Drape the rolled-out dough over your rolling pin and carefully slide it over all of the apples in the pan. Use a spoon to push the edges down into the pan, comfortably nestling all of the apples inside the dough.

10. Place the pan on a cookie sheet and bake in the oven for 25 minutes or until the top is golden brown. The cookie sheet will catch any juice that may spill over the pan.

11. Allow the pie to cool for 15 minutes in the pan. Meanwhile, reheat the caramel sauce over medium heat.

12. Place a plate over the pie. Using oven gloves because the pan will still be hot, flip the pie onto the plate in one fluid motion. Drizzle the caramel sauce over the pie and serve immediately with a large dollop of whipped cream.

HAZELNUT CHOC FROSTED SKILLET CAKE

COOK TIME: 35 MINS | MAKES: 6-8 SERVINGS

INGREDIENTS:

- 1 tbsp. butter
- 1 tsp. kosher salt
- 1 tsp. bicarbonate of soda
- 2 tsp. baking powder
- 2 1/2 cups cake flour
- 1 cup cocoa powder
- 1 1/2 cups white sugar
- 1/2 stick butter
- 1 cup buttermilk
- 2 tsp. vanilla essence
- 1/4 cup sunflower oil

- 3 large eggs
- For the Frosting:
- 1 tsp. vanilla essence
- 3 cups icing sugar
- 3/4 cups Nutella spread
- 1 stick butter, softened
- 1/4 cup heavy whipping cream

DIRECTIONS:

1. Set the oven to preheat at 350°F. Use 1 tablespoon butter to generously grease the inside of a 12-inch cast-iron pan.

2. Sift together the salt, bicarbonate of soda, baking powder, cake flour, and cocoa powder in a large bowl.

3. In a separate bowl, beat the sugar and butter until light and fluffy, incorporating as much air as possible.

4. Whisk together the buttermilk, vanilla, oil, and 3ggs in a separate bowl.

5. Alternating between the flour and the egg mixture gradually beat all of the ingredients into the butter. Beating for an additional 3 minutes to incorporate air.

6. Scrape the batter into your prepared pan and bake in the oven for 30-35 minutes or until an inserted skewer comes out clean.

7. Meanwhile, beat the vanilla, icing sugar, Nutella, and butter. When everything is properly combined, gradually beat in the heavy cream. Place the frosting in the fridge while the cake bakes.

8. Allow the cake to cool completely before frosting and serving.

PINEAPPLE TARTE TIN

COOK TIME: 50 MINS | MAKES: 6-8 SERVINGS

INGREDIENTS:

- 2 tbsp. butter
- 5 pineapple rings
- 1/2 tsp. kosher salt
- 2 tsp. bicarbonate of soda
- 2 tbsp. baking powder
- 2 tbsp. dark brown sugar
- 1 cup semolina flour
- 3 cups cake flour
- 1 lemon, zested
- 1 vanilla bean, halved and seeds scraped out
- 1 tsp. vanilla essence

- 3/4 cup sunflower oil
- 1 3/4 cups full-cream milk
- 1 cup sour cream
- 4 large eggs
- 2 tbsp. maraschino cherry juice
- 1/4 cup maraschino cherries
- 1 cup butter, softened
- raw honey

DIRECTIONS:

1. Set the oven to preheat at 375°F.

2. Melt the butter in a cast-iron skillet over medium heat. Once the butter is bubbling, add the pineapple rings and fry for 4-6 minutes or until the rings are golden brown, flipping once. Transfer the skillet to a wooden chopping board and set aside.

3. Sift together the salt, Bicarbonate of soda, baking powder, dark brown sugar, semolina flour, and cake flour in a large bowl.

4. In a separate bowl, beat the zest, vanilla bean, vanilla essence, oil, milk, sour cream, and eggs until properly combined. Fold in the flour mixture until everything is properly combined.

5. Gently scrape the batter over the pineapples in the skillet and smooth out the top. Place the skillet in the oven and bake for 35-40 minutes or until the top is golden brown.

6. Meanwhile, in a clean bowl, beat the maraschino cherry juice, maraschino cherries, and butter until light and fluffy. Place in the fridge until you need it.

7. Once the cake is done, allow it to cool in the pan for a few minutes before placing a plate on top of the cake and flipping in one fluid motion.

8. Spread the chilled cream over the cake and drizzle with honey before serving.

ONE-SKILLET CHOCOLATE CHIP COOKIE

COOK TIME: 30 MINS | MAKES: 6-8 SERVING

INGREDIENTS:

- 1 cup butter, room temperature
- 1/2 cup white sugar
- 1 cup dark brown sugar
- 2 large eggs
- 1 tsp. vanilla essence
- 2 cups semisweet chocolate chips
- 1 tsp. kosher salt
- 1 tsp. bicarbonate of soda
- 2 1/2 cups cake flour
- chocolate buttons

DIRECTIONS:

1. Set the oven to preheat at 375°F. Lightly spray a 12-inch cast-iron skillet.

2. Cream the butter, white sugar, and brown sugar in a large bowl, incorporating as much air as possible. Gradually beat in the eggs followed by the vanilla. Beat in the chocolate chips, salt, bicarbonate of soda, and cake flour to form a stiff dough.

3. Press the cookie dough into the prepared skillet and decorate with the chocolate buttons before baking in the oven for 30 minutes or until the cookie is golden brown and the edges are slightly darker.

4. Allow the cookie to sit in the pan for 15 minutes before slicing and serving.

CPSIA information can be obtained
at www.ICGtesting.com
Printed in the USA
BVHW050452121121
621276BV00003B/123

9 781922 590183